Teaching Every Child:

A Guide for Literacy Teams, Grades 1–3

Leslie Patterson
and
Frances Mallow

Christopher-Gordon Publishers, Inc.
Norwood, Massachusetts

Copyright Acknowledgments

Every effort has been made to contact copyright holders for permission to reproduce borrowed material where necessary. We apologize for any oversights and would be happy to rectify them in future printings.

Copyright © 2001 Christopher-Gordon Publishers, Inc.

All rights reserved. Except for review purposes, no part of this material protected by this copyright notice may be reproduced or utilized in any form or by any means, electronic or mechanical, including photocopying, recording, or any information and retrieval system, without the express written permission of the publisher or copyright holder.

The Bill Harp Professional Teacher's Library
An Imprint of
Christopher-Gordon Publishers, Inc.
1502 Providence Highway, Suite 12
Norwood, MA 02062
800-934-8322

Printed in the United States of America

10 9 8 7 6 5 4 3 2 1   05 04 03 02 01

Library of Congress Catalog Card Number: 2001-086214
ISBN: 1-929024-28-2

Dedication

To all reading and language arts teachers
who often feel as if they are between rocks
and hard places' working to help
students become joyfully literate.

Acknowledgments

This book comes from our ongoing friendships and collaboration with colleagues in public schools and universities in the Houston, Texas, area.

We particularly thank those who invited us onto their campuses as they worked together to build literacy teams. Thanks to faculties in Alief, at Alexander Elementary, in Conroe, at Travis Intermediate, Armstrong Elementary, and Giesinger Elementary; in Cypress Fairbanks, at Yeager Elementary and Holmsley Elementary; in Houston, at Travis Elementary, Deady Middle School, Mark Twain Elementary, and Milby High School; in Klein, at Klein Forest High School. On these campuses we found administrators and teachers working with courage and grace in the face of incredible challenges, including high stakes tests and intense public scrutiny.

We also learned side by side with outstanding graduate students at the University of Houston. Their continual questions and their classroom-based research kept us focused and moving forward. Diana Bernshausen, Carol Cotten, Barbara Jones, Sharon Lewis, Patty Oliver, Karen Palividas, Renee Rubin, Ruth Silva, Leigh Van Horn, and Joan Parker Webster generously shared their work with students and with teachers to learn more about how collaborative literacy teaching and learning can work.

Thanks also to Suzanne Canavan and Laurie Maker for their steady hands in moving this project forward. We also thank the anonymous reviewers for their perceptive insights and advice. This book is much more useful because of their input.

Finally, thanks to our families who are there when we need them and patiently wait as we work on the next project or deadline.

Contents

A Letter to Readers		ix
One	**Literacy Teams: Puzzling Over Kids' Needs**	1
	What? So What? and Now What? An Inquiry Cycle For Literacy Teams	2
	Forming Literacy Teams	4
	Questions for Dialogue	8
	Resources for Further Inquiry	8
Two	**Thinking about Support for Young Readers and Writers**	9
	What is Emerging Literacy?	9
	Thinking About Development	17
	Finding Reasons to Read and Write	20
	Questions for Further Dialogue	22
	Resources for Further Inquiry	25
Three	**Kids Who Just Sit and Watch**	27
	What is Happening?	27
	So What Does This Mean?	28
	Now What Shall We Do?	28
	Resources for Further Inquiry	31
Four	**Kids Who Don't Seem to Care**	33
	What Is Happening?	33
	So What Does This Mean?	34
	Now What Shall We Do?	34
	Resources for Further Inquiry	40
Five	**Kids Who Don't Know How Written Language Works**	41
	What Is Happening?	41
	So What Does This Mean?	42
	Now What Shall We Do?	42
	Resources for Further Inquiry	52
Six	**Kids Who Are Reluctant to Write**	53
	What Is Happening?	53
	So What Does This Mean?	54
	Now What Shall We Do?	54
	Resources for Further Inquiry	60
Seven	**Kids Who Don't Get The Big Picture When They Read**	61
	What Is Happening?	61
	So What Does This Mean?	62
	Now What Shall We Do?	62
	Resources for Further Inquiry	69

Eight	**Kids Who Don't Use Visual and Structural Cues To Make Meaning**	**71**
	What Is Happening?	71
	So What Does This Mean?	72
	Now What Shall We Do?	72
	Resources for Further Inquiry	86
Nine	**Kids Who Know About Letters and Sounds and Still Can't Read**	**87**
	What Is Happening?	88
	So What Does This Mean?	88
	Now What Shall We Do?	89
	Resources for Further Inquiry	95
Ten	**Kids Who Have Little Experience with "School English"**	**97**
	What Is Happening?	98
	So What Does This Mean?	98
	Now What Shall We Do?	98
	Resources for Further Inquiry	103
Eleven	**Solving Puzzles, Changing Lives**	**105**
References		**107**
About the Authors		**109**
Index		**111**

A Letter to Readers

Dear Readers,

In many countries, teachers and parents are fairly relaxed about how and when children begin to read. In fact, formal reading instruction in some eastern European countries doesn't begin until age seven.

But that is certainly not happening in the United States today. Teachers are bombarded with news reports about how children are simply not learning to read as well as they did in the past. The argument goes like this: The earlier we can begin to teach reading and the earlier we can "identify problems" and "intervene," the more our students will benefit. We disagree with this approach. We think that the best support we can give all children is rich and varied language and literacy experiences—reasons to become readers and writers. In that environment, informed teachers can teach what students need as they need it. But we must admit that politicians and business leaders seem to be in a panic about what we can do to make sure all children learn to read early and well.

That panic is spreading to homes and schools. In fact, we know a three-year-old who recently turned to her mom after watching an infomercial and asked for "Hooked on Phonics" because it was "time for me to learn to read." Mom laughed and told her not to worry—that she'd learn to read soon enough, reading bedtime stories and writing letters to Grandma. Shocked and hurt at Mom's reply, she ran crying to her bedroom. The marketing folks have done their jobs well.

Obviously, reading instruction is big business in U.S. homes and classrooms. Teachers feel pressure from all sides to make sure children learn to read early. Many teachers tell us that if children are not reading by the end of kindergarten, they will fall further and further behind the expectations imposed by mandated, high-stakes assessments at third and fourth grades. Kindergarten parents expect to see worksheets, basal readers, and spelling lists come home, and claims from quick-fix commercial programs add to this pressure.

All this is happening at a time when statistics and teachers' stories convince us that many children are coming to school with unprecedented emotional and physical needs. Many parents (often single parents) are struggling to provide food, adequate housing, and medical care. Even affluent families are striving to maintain some measure of emotional stability and a stable family life. When children are hungry or cold, frightened or upset, they find it difficult to focus on literacy tasks at school.

Teachers we know are doing their best to meet these significant needs in the face of the mounting pressure that all children—regardless of other needs—be fluent and proficient readers by seven years of age. To respond to that pressure, we suggest that teachers make two critical professional moves. First, they should learn as much as possible about language and literacy—so that they have a realistic idea about the range of typical literacy behaviors among young children (who are, we must remind ourselves, only 60–80 months of age). This knowledge helps us build confidence in our decisions, maintain a sensible perspective, and sustain our energy and enthusiasm for teaching and learning. This knowledge also helps us talk to parents, to administrators, and to children about realistic expectations.

Second, teachers should also refine their problem-solving strategies for spotting a child's strengths, building on those strengths, and responding appropriately. We should consider what that child needs to learn next and what the most supportive instruction might be. In the best of all possible worlds, teams of teachers do this puzzle-solving together, systematically looking for ways to help one another and to draw on a wide range of campus and community resources to support their children. As colleagues, we can work together to support struggling students, to broaden our children's support networks to include the librarian, the counselors, other school staff, parents, and concerned neighbors in the community.

We are seeing this kind of collaborative problem-solving become systematic and powerful through the implementation of Literacy Teams on campuses across the country (Lewis, 2000). Through Literacy Teams, teachers can work together to support these children in more powerful ways than any single teacher could hope to do. We wrote this book to help teachers, parents, reading specialists, counselors, and principals work together in this collaborative, puzzle-solving process.

Chapter 1 gives suggestions about how to begin Literacy Teams on your campus. These teams will work differently on each campus. Sometimes they are formal committees, with regular meetings and designated representatives from each grade level. Sometimes they are grade level teams of teachers who routinely talk about children who need extra help. Sometimes they are study groups that meet during staff development times, to learn more about literacy teaching and learning, to try research-based strategies that promise to meet the needs of particular students.

Chapter 2 provides an overview of emergent literacy, a framework for primary teachers to use as they think about what they want to see their children doing and about how to support early literacy learning.

In chapters 3–10, we focus on particular concerns teachers have for struggling emergent readers and writers, suggesting some assessment and instructional strategies to use with these kids who puzzle us. We must say that these concerns—these puzzles—do not always signal that something has gone "wrong." Sometimes what we are seeing are typical developmental behaviors for children just learning to read and write; these children simply need rich literacy opportunities and support from knowledgeable teachers and parents. Sometimes what they need is more time and experience as they learn the complexities of written language. Given the external pressure teachers are feeling, it may be hard to relax and give those students time to emerge as literate and confident learners. We hope this book and your colleagues can help you decide how you can best support each of your students as you solve these literacy puzzles together.

Sincerely,

Leslie and Frances

Chapter 1

Literacy Teams: Puzzling Over Kids' Needs

When I asked Suzanne, "Are you a good reader?" her answer puzzled me. She said "yes" and was unable to tell me what a good reader does or why another student was a good reader. I know I have modeled what a good reader does both in large and small group settings, but she was unable to recall anything that would make someone a good reader. I admit I am confused and puzzled. . . .

*****

David reads with me two–three days a week from a book he has chosen, but he struggles with the sounds in English (for example, he says "Ee" for the word "I"). He stays focused during our reading time together and even with a large group. We have made some flash cards with sight words on them, but I made the mistake of sending that set home. (They never got back to school.) He is a delight to work with, but he's just not moving into more difficult texts.

*****

Ramon was reading at Level 13 in the guided reading group, struggling with unfamiliar words and having a hard time making sense of the books. And then, last week, I noticed that during social studies time he was reading silently in a book that was at least Level 20. I sat down with him and asked him to read a couple pages out loud and tell me about it. He understood it just fine! Now what is that about?

These are voices of teachers who, like millions of others across the country, are working hard to help all their students be successful. The difference for these teachers is that they come together routinely to problem-solve about how to help all their students become independent, proficient, and enthusiastic readers and writers. These teachers work together in a campus Literacy Team—a small group of teachers committed to ensuring literacy success for all their students.

A Literacy Team may be operating on your campus as a "child study team," or an "instructional assistance team." You may be lucky enough to have two or three colleagues with whom you meet regularly to talk about your kids and what they need. If you (and your students) are very fortunate, you have a principal who understands that time is essential, a principal who builds time into your school days for systematic collaborative problem solving and planning. These are Literacy Teams. Sometimes these Literacy Teams not only talk about issues related to individual children, but they also begin looking at campus-wide issues. At that point, they ask questions about curriculum—questions like these

- What are the strengths and needs among all our third graders?
- How do our teachers know which books to use with which students?
- What literacy performances do we expect from students who move from one grade level to the next?

We suggest that you keep a journal so that you can record what you notice about your students and about yourself as you try the ideas presented throughout this book. Your journal provides a "paper trail" for you to retrace your decisions, to see what came before so you can make sense of what comes later. We like to keep our journals in two columns—one for our observations and one for our reflections and comments. Sometimes it's hard to keep those separate, but we have found it helpful to be able to point to what really happened and separate that from our wonderings and conclusions about what it means.

What? So What? Now What?
An Inquiry Cycle for Literacy Teams

We suggest an inquiry cycle used by many teacher researchers we know:

- *What* is happening?
- *So what* does that mean?
- *Now what* shall I do about it?

Those three questions move in and out of teacher researchers' reflections and

WHAT is happening?

NOW WHAT are we going to do about it?

SO WHAT does it mean?

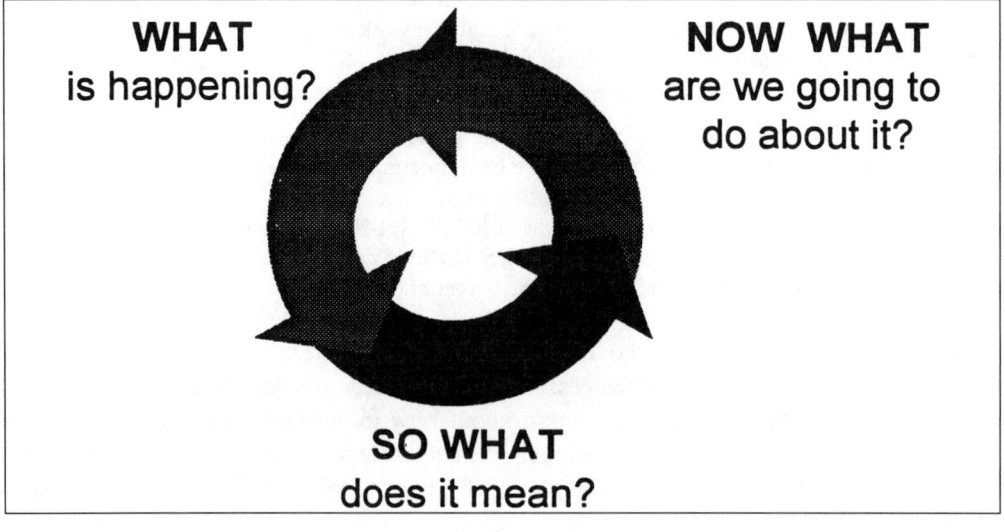

Figure 1.1 Action research cycle for Literacy Teams.

conversations, prompting us to let go of outdated assumptions and pushing us toward new understandings based on our students' responses and published research. Figure 1.2 lists other questions that fit into this simple cycle.

What is happening?
- What is happening in my classroom?
- How are my students responding?
- What puzzles or paradoxes do I see?
- Who seems to be struggling?
- Which students am I concerned about?
- What is happening with them?
- What, specifically, are they doing as they read? As they write?
- What do they say about their reading and writing?

So what does that mean?
- What are the beliefs and guiding principles that drive my decisions?
- What past experiences seem to influence my students' responses?
- What are my students' strengths?
- What are their targets for growth?
- What does that mean for my teaching targets?
- What do my students behaviors and comments related to reading and writing imply about their self-confidence? About their attitudes toward literacy? About their risk-taking?

Now what am I going to do about it?
- What do my students need next?
- What resources do I need to serve their needs?
- How am I going to change my teaching in response to what my students are learning?
- What am I learning about language and literacy?
- Am I having to rethink what I thought I knew?
- How can I work more closely with the families of my students?
- How can I invite my students into this inquiry?
- What new questions do I have?
- How can I begin to answer those questions?

Figure 1.2 Questions to guide Literacy Team dialogue and inquiry.

This dialogue and inquiry process, one form of action research, is not a neat step-by-step process. It's dynamic, complex, and messy. Through action research, teachers, parents, and students can combine action, reflection, dialogue, and inquiry to focus on particular problems for particular students. As we continue, both individually and together, to ask questions and look for answers, we will make discoveries and find new questions, questions that drive further reflection and problem-solving. This "What? So what? Now what?" process can become an ongoing, transformative experience for everyone.

If you are also reading what other researchers have to say and are asking "What? So what? and Now what?" about published findings from other classrooms, your new understandings will be even more solidly grounded in what we are all learning about how children become literate in our schools. That is why we have listed readings at the end of each chapter.

Another way we can think about this cycle of reflection, inquiry, dialogue, and action is to focus on what teachers do as they problem-solve. They look and listen in their classrooms, trying to observe closely—to see and hear exactly what their children do and say as they read and write. Then teachers talk to one another and think about what it all means. Soon—sometimes immediately, they must act. Teachers cannot afford the luxury of long reflections in solitude. They must act and act quickly to respond to students' needs. Figure 1.3 shows one way to think about how reflective teachers and teacher researchers work.

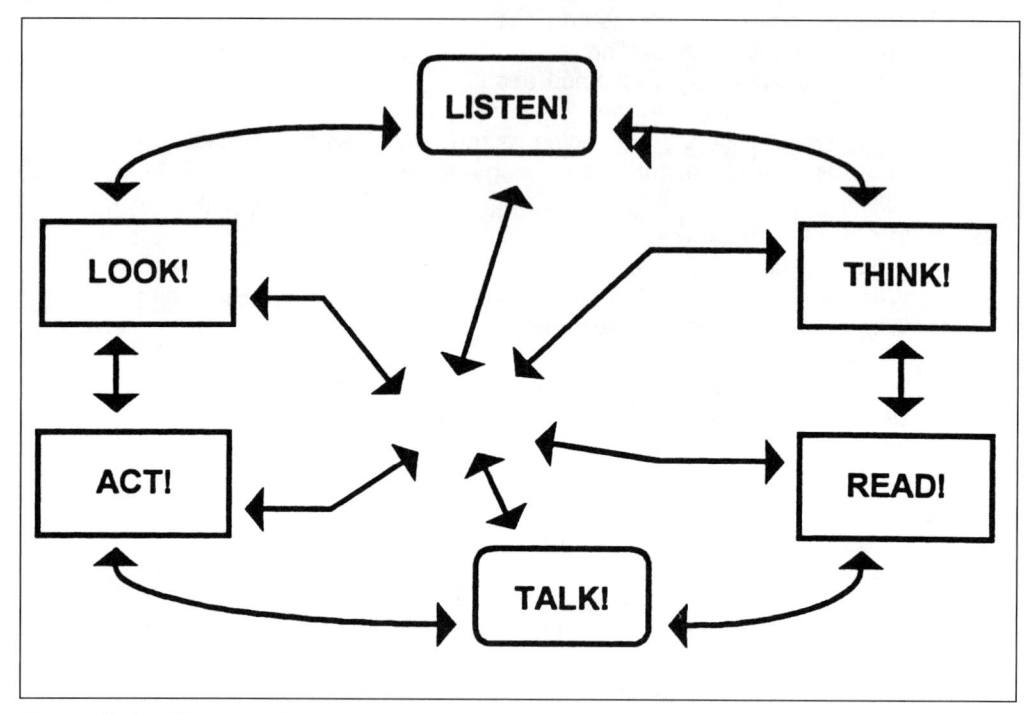

Figure 1.3 What teachers do in Literacy Teams.

Forming Literacy Teams

We have watched and worked with Literacy Teams in several schools in and around Houston, Texas. It's no surprise that each one is unique. The team at Alexander Elementary in Alief, Texas, began as a group of reading specialists and teachers committed to schoolwide innovation based on the best research in reading and writing instruction. With a great deal of support from the principal and from the district Reading/Language Arts Director, these teachers focused lots of time and energy on learning everything they could about how to support young children in their reading and writing. Soon it became apparent that they needed a vertical team, so that they could make plans across grade levels. Not long after that, it was clear that the focus needed to broaden even more, beyond reading and writing, to include math and inquiry across the content areas. At Alexander, high expectations for children and high expectations for teachers to continue their professional development became part of the campus culture. Teachers who didn't buy into the philosophy began asking for transfers, and new teachers made a conscious choice to join that learning team.

Our commitment to the Literacy Team process has been strengthened as we have watched faculties from Alexander Elementary, Armstrong and Giesinger Elementary Schools in Conroe, Texas, and Washington Intermediate in Conroe, Texas. We have watched these faculties work through this process for about three years, in a sincere and enthusiastic effort to support their struggling readers and writers and to build vibrant learning communities. As we have worked with teachers in these inquiry teams or study groups, we have found that, to be successful, we need to make sure certain conditions are in place:

- *Trust*—All participants must trust one another enough to take interpersonal and professional risks. In productive groups, we see strong personal bonds, even friendships, emerging from the collaborative work.
- *Time*—Time for inquiry and for discussion must be built into the school day, integrated into the culture of the school.
- *Task*—Teachers must have a shared concern, some shared understandings about research-based instruction, and a concrete task that brings them together for the good of their students.
- *Talk*—Dialogue (both written and oral) provides a critical vehicle for making shared thinking visible.
- *Text*—Artifacts, documents, and test data all provide examples of student work—concrete representation of student responses and a focus for talking about how kids are doing.

As you join with other teachers to form Literacy Teams (or whatever you choose to call your group), this book can serve as a road map to suggest directions for your collaborative inquiry. Here are some suggestions about how to get started:

- Set up a regular meeting time, as often as you can afford the time. Every two weeks works for most groups. Some teachers find that after school is a good time. Or you may want to form a "breakfast club" to meet at the beginning of the day, when you are fresh. Sometimes your group shares a planning period, and you can find time during the school day to get together. Some campuses have found ways to bring substitutes in for a few hours every couple weeks, or they use volunteers to work with students to give teachers time to work together periodically.
- Choose someone to be the facilitator and someone to be the recorder, at least for the first few meetings. You may want to take turns with those jobs, but it helps to get into a routine. Remember that this works best if you try to focus your discussion on the issues at hand. This is not a time for unfocused conversations, as much fun as that may be.
- Have the recorder keep notes of each meeting, and, if possible, make copies available to everyone. After a couple months of meetings you will be glad to be able to look back on these notes to see where your inquiry has gone.
- Talk about "ground rules" for your conversations. Here are a few examples:
    - Keep the negative talk to a minimum, because this is not the time for complaining or blaming.
    - Listen carefully to others.
    - Make sure everyone gets a chance to contribute.
    - Comments made here are confidential and will be shared only if they can help get a child the support she needs.
- Talk about what you want to accomplish with these meetings. Set the agenda for the next discussion at the end of each meeting, and think about what each of you will do in the meantime. For example, what does each person agree to bring to the next meeting?

Figures 1.4 and 1.5 are examples of planning sheets that may help you decide how to begin your collaborative inquiry.

As we try to make sure our students learn what they need to know before they go on to

---

Literacy Team Plan

Group Members:

Our Goal(s):

Our Ground Rules:

Tentative Meeting Times:

Figure 1.4 Literacy Team planning sheet.

the next grade, this Literacy Team process serves us well. What works with one child falls flat with another. What works one year is useless the next year. We are constantly having to look for better answers to new questions. That search for better answers feeds our classroom decisions and actions. It also helps us build our personal theories, that, in turn, guide and inform our decisions about our students.

When people first learn about Literacy Teams and action research in schools, they often ask what is so special about it. It just seems like common sense. Action research just seems to be what good teachers have done for years, and, in a way, that's true. All good

Literacy Team Minutes

Date:

Facilitator:

Recorder:

Participants:

Agenda:

Insights from the Discussion:

New Questions:

Next Action Step(s):

Next Meeting—Date/Place/Facilitator:

Figure 1.5 Literacy Team Minutes.

teachers think about their decisions—they gather information about what their students are learning, and they use that information to make new decisions. They reflect on what works and what doesn't work. But Literacy Teams and collaborative action research can even improve the work of good teachers. Collaborative work like this goes beyond "good teaching" because of its systematic data gathering and analysis. Teacher researchers can explain what they have learned and how they learned it. They also develop a "paper trail" that helps others learn from their research. These teachers can use their findings to make better decisions tomorrow, and they can also share their findings with colleagues down the hall or across the country.

Teaching is not just a matter of telling students what they need to know. It is not just a matter of delivering information or guiding students to new discoveries. Teaching is also learning. It is a responsive and dynamic process driven by questions about how students learn and how we can best help them. This teaching/learning process helps us continually reinvent what learning looks like in our classrooms and transforms who we are as teachers and learners.

More Questions for Dialogue

- Who is one student whose literacy progress has you puzzled? What do you see him or her doing? Why are you puzzled or worried about that?
- Who are the students across your campus who seem to be the most successful learners? What do they have in common?
- Who are the students across your campus who seem to be struggling? What strengths do they have that could serve as a springboard for their progress?
- What does it mean to be literate on your campus? What do you and your colleagues value in terms of literacy attitudes and behaviors?

Resources for Further Inquiry

Allington, R, & Walmsley, S. (Eds.). (1995). *No quick fix: Rethinking literacy programs in American elementary schools.* New York: Teachers College Press; Newark, DE: International Reading Association.

Birchak, B. (1998). *Teacher study groups: Building community through dialogue and reflection.* Urbana, IL: National Council of Teachers of English.

Calkins, L. (1999). *A teacher's guide to standardized reading tests: Knowledge is power.* Portsmouth, NH: Heinemann.

Coles, G. (1998). *Reading lessons: The debate over literacy.* New York: Hill and Wang.

Donoahue, Z., Van Tassell, M., & Patterson, L. (1996). *Texts, talk, and inquiry.* Newark, DE: International Reading Association.

Delpit, L. (1995). *Other people's children: Cultural conflict in the classroom.* New York: New Press.

Goodman, K. (1996). *On reading.* Portsmouth, NH: Heinemann.

Harwayne, S. (1999). *Going public: Priorities & practice at the Manhattan New School.* Portsmouth, NH: Heinemann.

Lewis, S. (2000). *Evolution of a Reading Recovery© literacy team: A systemic, schoolwide approach to early intervention.* An unpublished doctoral dissertation, University of Houston.

Mallow, F., & Patterson, L. (1999). *Framing literacy: Teaching/learning in K–8 classrooms.* Norwood, MA: Christopher-Gordon.

McQuillan, J. (1998). *The literacy crisis: False claims, real solutions.* Portsmouth, NH: Heinemann.

Stephens, D., & Storey, J. (1999). *Assessment as inquiry: Learning the hypothesis-test process.* Urbana, IL: National Council of Teachers of English.

Chapter 2

Thinking About Support for Young Readers and Writers

As a primary teacher you already know about what happens as children learn to read and write. You know how to build a supportive and literacy rich classroom environment. You know that children need a predictable routine and that they need to talk and listen to one another. You know they need to listen and respond to wonderful literature written for children.

You also know that literacy takes more time and comes harder for some children than for others. Literacy learning, much like physical growth, happens in spurts and plateaus. It does not make sense to expect that all children at 72 months of age will be reading and writing exactly the same. As a teacher, the trick is to know when to offer support and when to intervene in support of this individualistic development and learning. As you and your colleagues work together to offer extra support for the students whose progress is puzzling you, it is helpful for you to start with some common understandings about what literacy is and about how people become literate. You may not agree on all the details (researchers and other folks outside the classroom certainly don't), but it helps to have common vocabulary and agreement on a few basic issues. The following is a very brief discussion of what we know about emergent literacy. Check the readings at the end of the chapter for suggestions for more detailed discussions.

What is Emergent Literacy?

When does literacy begin? In a literate society such as ours, the process of becoming literate begins early in life. As a child acquires and develops oral language, the interrelated literacy processes of reading and writing are also developing. Just as very young children play an active, constructive role in their own language acquisition, they also play an active, constructive role in their own literacy development. The term, emergent literacy, in wide use today, generally means "the reading and writing behaviors of young children that precede and develop into conventional literacy" (Sulzby, 1989).

Emergent literacy refers to the kinds of behaviors children exhibit when they are beginning to notice that talk can be written down and that patterns in text have some sort of meaning. At this point, they still depend on pictures and colors as meaning cues, but they are learning more and more about how printed words represent spoken language—on signs along the road and in storybooks at bedtime. Environmental print—the McDonald's golden arches and the Nike swoosh—are important sources of meaning and provide bridges to more abstract text—letters and words and sentences. Emergent readers and writers make important decisions about what they want to say (through pictures and their approximations of conventional writing) in a letter to grandmother or in a sign on the bedroom door or on a name tag on a favorite coat.

The emergence of oral language takes place in an environment that facilitates each attempt at meaning. . . . an environment where parents and caretakers respond to language attempts with encouragement and do whatever it takes to facilitate these attempts (Wells, 1981). The support and encouragement takes the forms of accepting all attempts at language, often with much celebration and hand clapping! Adults adjust their language when interacting with young children, using simple words and much repetition. Within this nurturing environment, it is safe for children to engage in the risky business of constructing their knowledge of oral language and trying it out. As they try it out in various social situations, they come to understand how they can use it and how it can be used by others.

Engagement in meaning-making takes place as life is lived. In the course of the day-to-day social living in a family, surrounded by language embedded in purposeful situations, the child experiences language used in multiple ways for multiple purposes. The development of language occurs with each attempt to engage in acts of communication, both as a receiver and a producer of language. Thus, oral language development takes place within social interactions in which language is used purposefully and meaningfully to get something done.

Like oral language events, literacy events are also mostly social. Oral language and literacy exist so that meaning can be created and communicated between and among humans. Also, like oral language events, literacy events have many uses and functions. Young children often participate in literacy events in their homes. Research by Teale (1986) in low income homes with children who were 2 1/2 to 3 1/2 years old identified nine domains of human activity in which reading and writing took place:

- in daily living routines;
- as a source of entertainment;
- in school-related activities such as playing school or homework done by older siblings;
- in events directly related to work or securing work;
- in religious practices;
- through interpersonal communication such as note and letter writing;
- through information networks within the community;
- during storybook time; and
- for the sake of teaching or learning, such as teaching a child to write his/her name.

This and other research gives us is rich evidence that demonstrations of literacy take place in most homes, regardless of economic status.

The emergence of literacy begins much as the emergence of oral language begins. . . with the need to make meaning (Halliday, 1973). Research on the emergence of literacy has concentrated on three areas: environmental print, storybook reading, and the development of writing. We will briefly explore each of these.

Environmental Print

The research studies of environmental print have shown us that even very young children learn about written language from their environment (Goodman, 1980; Harste, Woodward, and Burke, 1984). All children encounter print in the environment. From the print on the Pampers package to the golden arches of McDonald's, environmental print provides encounters with written language. It is a very important source of information about print for young children. Through their use and understanding of environmental print, they learn words, they learn how written language works—they learn that it is meaningful, and that it is used to get things done. Again, within the context of daily living, children as young as 15 to 18 months old construct their own knowledge about environmental print as a tool to get what they want. They use this knowledge when they point to a fast food sign and ask for french fries, when they point to the correct box in the pantry and ask for crackers, and when they point to the Band-Aid box after Mom has cleaned and applied ointment to a scrape.

Storybook Reading

Researchers like Sulzby (1985) have taught us that the highly contextualized identification of environmental print is far different from reading of continuous text, as found in storybook reading. Through storybook reading, young children learn and experience many things. Probably the two most important things are that they learn what readers do and they learn how text works (Hall, 1987).

As parents and other caregivers read to children, they engage in conversations, answer questions, and respond to statements. These experiences often lead a child to understand that the message is carried in the print; that books are read front to back, line by line, word by word; that print is different from pictures; that there are relationships between the words spoken and the print observed; that print is made up of letters, words, punctuation, and spaces; and that there is a language associated with the activity of reading books—such as page, front, back, word, and so forth.

Through hearing stories read aloud, even very young children gain an understanding of how written language works, especially storybook language. Though storybook reading may start out with very young children as a totally interactive process, the process becomes less interactive and more verbatim reading as the child is able to sit still longer and focus attention for longer periods of time. They know when Dad has skipped a page or two when reading a favorite bedtime story, and they may even have memorized favorite books. Through continued experience with repeated readings, this book language often shows up in their play as they use phrases such as "Once upon a time," "he huffed and he puffed," and "The end." Many children reenact stories in their play. As they internalize story structure, they are able to use this knowledge in telling their own stories. The ability to tell their own stories, to create "sustained talk" seems to be facilitated by storybook reading and is a strong predictor of literacy success in school.

Writing Development

Children have been observed to write in emergent forms as soon as they could hold a crayon and make a mark on paper. Focusing on the forms that emergent writing may take, Sulzby and Teale (1985) collected evidence that children's writing may go through a pattern of development that moves from less to more sophisticated strategies and knowledge.

The developmental sequence has been described as scribbling, drawing, nonphonetic letter strings, invented spelling, and conventional writing. This developmental sequence is not a linear, straightforward process, but rather it is recursive, with a child revisiting and using old forms while trying out new knowledge. Mallow (1993) also observed kindergarten students using drawing as an early form of writing. After only a few months in kindergarten, however, the students distinguished between their drawing and writing.

Harste, Woodward, and Burke (1984) examined young children's writing within a literacy event and stated that each writing event also involved speaking, listening, and reading. They found recurring patterns that seem to explain that young children use the same literacy processes that adults use. Even very young children have to make organizational decisions as they write. They write, in whatever form, with intention of meaning and each transaction with writing leads to new constructions of meaning. These researchers found risk-taking in writing as central to cognitive processing and viewed all literacy development in light of social situations and context. They found that any text produced by children was viewed as having meaning and that learning took place within demonstrations that were made available through social participation with others.

It seems clear, from research and from personal experience, that most children entering kindergarten today know that writing is a meaningful activity used to communicate messages. They also know that written language is composed of elements and has forms and structures. They may be exploring the various uses of language in their writing to accomplish different purposes. In her work with kindergarten students, Mallow (1993) found that they use writing to get what they want, to initiate or maintain social relationships, to express their feelings, to give information, to record in order to remember, to pretend, and to direct the actions of someone else.

To sum up the major understandings that have come from research on the literacy of very young children, Teale and Sulzby (1989) found six general conclusions:

- Children in a literate society begin learning to read and write very early in life.
- The young child's reading and writing abilities are interrelated processes that develop concurrently rather than sequentially.
- The child develops as a reader/writer in an intimate connection with the development of oral language. So the child is developing as a reader/writer/speaker with each role supporting the other.
- Learning to read and write requires active participation in activities that have meaning in the child's daily life. Literacy develops out of real life settings in which reading and writing are used to get things done. The functions of literacy seem to be as much a part of learning to read and write as are the formal aspects of written language.
- Young children are actively involved in the process of their own literacy development and social interaction with responsive others plays a key role in this process. Through observation of others' literacy and being able to explore written language on their own, young children construct their own understandings and skills in reading and writing.
- Being read to plays a special role in the literacy development of the young child.

Characteristics of Emerging Literacy

We cannot over emphasize the power of "kidwatching" as Yetta Goodman (1978) pointed out so many years ago. When teachers know how to watch young readers and writers, when they know what to watch for, and how to respond when they see particular behaviors, they can individualize their teaching decisions for each learner. Many books are available to literacy teachers who want to know how to observe and assess emergent readers and writers. Check the titles at the end of this chapter, if you are interested in learning more about assessment.

We think it is important to remember that literacy is just one aspect of a young child's life and learning. In *Framing Literacy* (Mallow and Patterson, 1999), we suggest a framework for literacy assessment that encourages teachers, parents, and learners to look at the big literacy picture. Here are the five "frames" we suggest teachers use to organize their looking and listening in their literacy classrooms:

Frame 1: *Self-Efficacy*—refers to a child's willingness to face new challenges. She may be an active learner on the playground or in the block center, but passive when it is time to read and write. It's important for children to learn to take the risks inherent in reading and writing. They need to know that it's okay to make mistakes when you are learning to do something. In fact, they need to understand that mistakes can actually help you as you learn to do something new. The question teachers can ask themselves related to Frame 1 is this: To what extent are learners eager or passive readers and writers?

> **Frame 1:** To what extent are learners eager or passive readers and writers?

Frame 2: *World Knowledge*—refers to the range and depth of what a child knows about the world. A child whose family travels, attends public events, visits museums and art galleries will have much more knowledge about the wider world than other children. Of course, that is a middle-class experience of the world. A child who cooks and takes care of animals, who translates for her parents at social service agencies, who makes regular trips to Mexico to see her extended family also has a great deal of world knowledge. That child, however, may need a teacher to help make connections between her world knowledge and the knowledge typically valued in the school culture. The important point here is that good readers know about the world we read about in trade books and textbooks, magazines, and newspapers. Good readers also know how to use their background knowledge to make sense when they read and write. The question teachers ask themselves as they observe young students in Frame 2 is this: What do learners know about the world that can help them make sense of what they are reading and writing?

> **Frame 2:** What do learners know about the world that can help them make sense of what they are reading and writing?

Frame 3: *Literacy Knowledge and Strategies*—refers to what we typically think of as the basis of the literacy curriculum. Frame 3 is all about how children use letters, sounds, words, and other characteristics of print to make sense as they read or write. Frame 3 refers to what they know about how written language works, as well as what they can do with that knowledge.

Figure 2.2 represents what we understand about how proficient reading works. It illustrates what we are trying to help young children learn to do. Here's an explanation:

When we read, we use messages or cues in the text to make predictions or anticipate what particular words are and what ideas the author is trying to represent. Reading and writing are essentially prediction processes, or hypothesis testing processes. After we make a prediction, we confirm or disconfirm that prediction; we respond to the meanings; and then we integrate that bit of information into our prior knowledge and go on to sample more cues and make more predictions (Clay, 1998; Goodman, 1996).

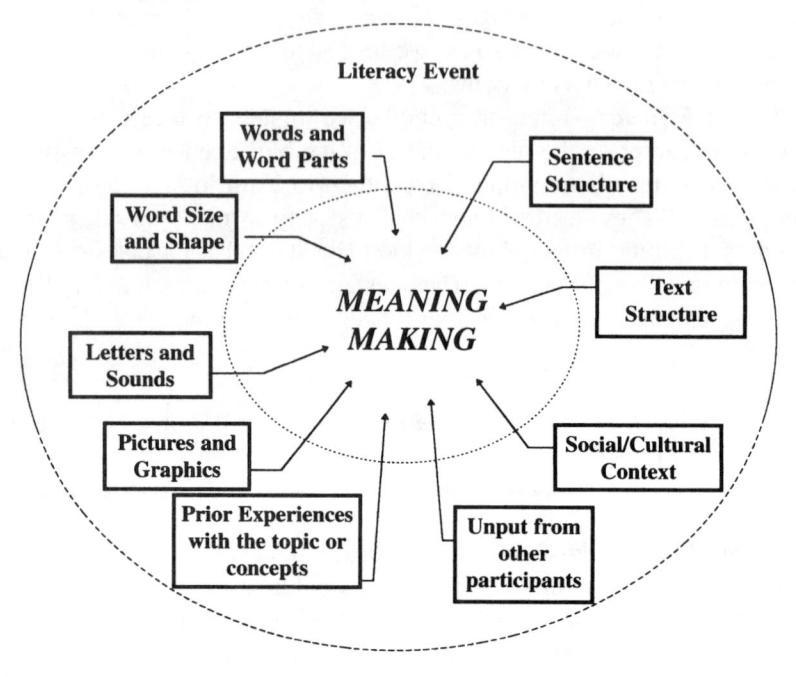

Figure 2.1 Cues readers and writers use to make meaning.

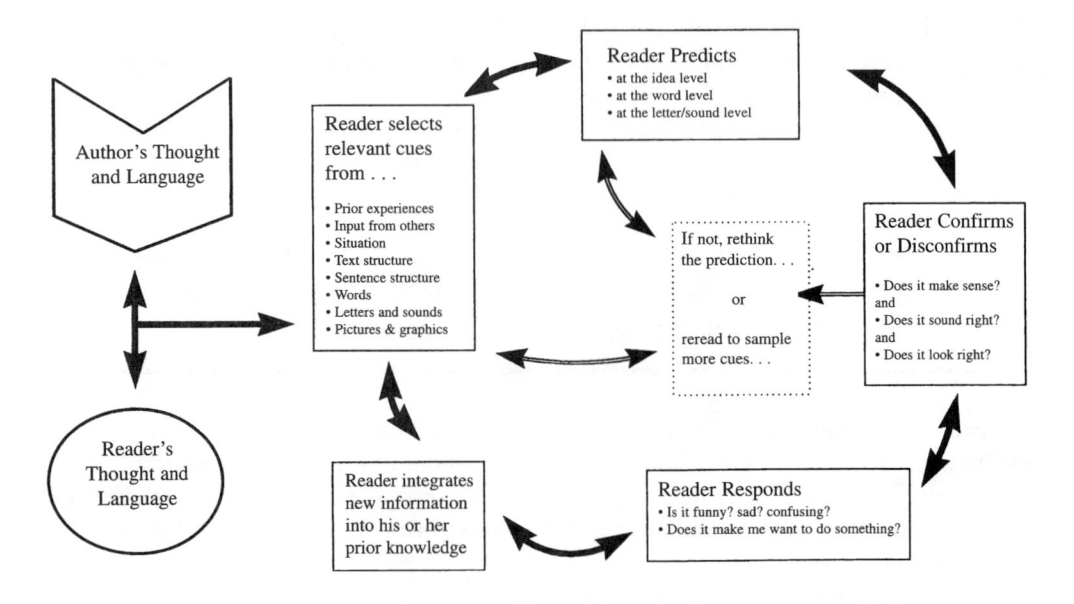

Figure 2.2 Proficient reading as a prediction cycle.

Good readers pay attention to the way language sounds. They learn that spoken language can be separated into sounds (phonemic awareness.) They learn that letters, words, and pictures "say" things when we read. They learn to use these cues, in addition to the syntax, word meanings, and cues about what the whole message might say. Good readers connect these cues to their background knowledge of the topic, the writer, and the situation as they read. Emergent readers can do that process pretty well already, as they "read" or "make meaning" of their parents' facial expressions or the pictures in books and on television.

As they learn more about the characteristics of written language, they apply this same meaning-making process to print. They gradually learn to pay attention to letter shapes, initial letters/sounds, patterns in words, and the words that represent familiar concepts. It is particularly important for them to write messages because, in writing, they can pay close attention to the way letters and sounds make words that mean something. As they read easy books with lots of repeated patterns and familiar concepts, they become more and more fluent with this process and can move into more difficult text. They learn which cues are important, and they learn to use those cues to infer and predict, to self monitor and try alternative readings when things don't make sense or don't sound right. They learn to remember what they are reading so they can use that information to make new inferences and predictions.

Look again at Figures 2.1 and 2.2 as you think about your own students and how they are reading. Your role is to support this process—to make sure students move through this process as they read and write, to offer hints and ask questions that help the reader use cues to make sense. When you are available to them during Sustained Silent Reading, Assisted Reading, or Guided Reading, you can do just that. In Frame 3, you ask this question: How do children use letters, sounds, words, and other characteristics of print to make sense as they read or write?

> **Frame 3:** How do children use letters, sounds, words, and other characteristics of print to make sense as they read or write?

Frame 4: *Reflection*—refers to whether emergent readers and writers can talk about what they are doing when they read and write. Can they point to the part of the page that tells the story? Can they tell why the word "house" is different from the word "horse"? Can they tell you what a good reader does when he comes to something hard? The primary question teachers ask in reference to Frame 4 is this: What can learners say about how and why they read and write the way they do?

> **Frame 4:** What can learners say about how and why they read and write the way they do?

Frame 5: *Functional and Critical Literacy*—refers to how an emergent reader uses literacy for authentic purposes. As a teacher observes young children, it is important to try to determine whether they know that reading and writing can accomplish things in the world outside the classroom. In assessing Frame 5, the teacher asks this question: How does the learner put literacy to work in his or her world? Several researchers have documented the "functions of language and literacy," although they may use slightly different terminology. We have used the work of Halliday (1973) and Smith (1982) in Table 2.1 to think about why children use language and what that might mean for the classroom:

Table 2.1 Why children use language and what that might mean for the classroom.

Function	Meaning	School Tasks
Instrumental	"I want . . ."	• Letters and notes • Lists
Regulatory	"Do this . . ."	• Letters and notes • Signs
Interactional	"Let's talk . . ."	• Letters and notes • Signs • Instructions
Personal	"Here I am . . ."	• Journals and diaries • Letters and notes • Art work
Heuristic	"I wonder . . ."	• Learning logs • Inquiry projects
Imaginative	"What if . . ."	• Stories • Poems and plays • Art work
Representational	"This is what I know . . ."	• Reports • Art work • Charts and graphs
Divertive	"Let's have fun . . ."	• Jokes and riddles • Songs • Poems • Games
Authoritative/Contractual	"This is how you do it . . ."	• Contracts • Instructions
Perpetuating	"This is how we will remember . . ."	• Journals • Reports • Memoirs • Biographies

Of course, teachers can plan instruction that leads students toward these tasks and products, but literacy rich classrooms also provide enough flexibility and time for students to generate ideas like this on their own.

> **Frame 5:** How does the learner put literacy to work in his or her world?

Thinking About Development

Research done in several languages suggests that learning to read and write is a developmental process for young children that can be generalized into stages or phases that children pass through in a variety of ways and at different stages in their attempts to comprehend or produce written language. Within this developmental process, there are fluctuations, regressions, and differences in children's attendance to and use of aspects of written language.

The list in Figure 2.3 suggests behaviors that teachers have noticed among readers and writers who seem to be "emerging" into literacy. Some kindergarten and first-grade teachers use lists like this to document children's growth over time. The important thing to remember is that we should always look for strengths and potentials for growth. If we focus only on what kids can't yet do, we send them and their parents the wrong message. Lists like this should not be used to identify "deficits" that require "remediation," but to provide signposts to decide where kids are and what support they might need next.

Behaviors that Demonstrate Emergent Literacy

Frame 1: Self Efficacy

- "Plays around" with language
- Shows an interest in books and pictures
- Shows "phonemic awareness," or the ability to identify and isolate sounds in spoken language, as well as to blend sounds into spoken words
- Is developing an interest in writing his/her name
- Likes to reread favorite books
- Looks at books and names pictures
- Is confident in making attempts at "reading"
- Is willing to experiment with writing using scribbles, one or two labels for pictures, and strings of letters
- Wants to read and write
- Is willing to share writing
- Self-selects books to sit and look at alone or to "read" to dolls or toys
- Is interested in listening to and telling in stories, poems, and rhymes

Frame 2: World Knowledge

- Makes connections with known world and books
- Knows environmental print and makes connections, such as associating McDonald's with french fries
- Knows names of letters, especially those in his/her name

Continued . . .

Figure 2.3 Behaviors that demonstrate emergent literacy.

- Is learning and recognizing book language and uses in play and retellings
- Remembers and uses known words and phrases from books in writing
- Writes about events in own life and interests

Frame 3: Literacy Knowledge and Strategies
- Understands top to bottom, left to right order of reading and writing
- Often memorizes stories that have been listened to repeatedly
- "Reads" by looking at the pictures
- Can retell a story in sequence
- Predicts by looking at the pictures
- After a fairly predictable sequence of writing development of scribbles, letter-like forms, and strings of letters, some sound symbol correspondence develops while writing, mainly beginning consonants, and this carries over into reading
- Often cannot reread writing after time has elapsed
- Copies words from other sources to use in writing
- Begins to realize that print is not arbitrary and that the meaning is carried in print
- Chimes in while listening to a familiar story
- Begins to supply missing words in familiar text
- Begins to focus on the print
- First reading may be own writing
- Voice, finger, and print match develops and oral reading is slow, word for word, often in a monotone
- All reading is oral in order to hear self read
- Begins to have a sight vocabulary in different contexts
- Is able to self-correct in reading and writing occasionally in order to maintain meaning
- Listening vocabulary and comprehension is far above reading

Frame 4: Reflection
- May be able to talk about why certain books are favorites
- Talks while writing

Frame 5: Functional and Critical Literacy
- Uses knowledge of environmental print to get what he/she wants in the grocery store, at fast food restaurants
- May use his/her own form of writing to leave messages for family members
- May use his/her own form of writing to establish ownership

Figure 2.3 (*Continued*) Behaviors that demonstrate emergent literacy.

Moving Toward Fluency

Many young children move through emergent literacy behaviors very quickly. Some are reading conventionally by the time they are 6 or 7 years old. As they begin using all the available cues in more strategic ways, as they learn more and more words, and as they begin reading and writing a wide variety of texts, they exhibit what we can call fluent meaning-making. This is not the same as "fluent" oral reading, that means few or no mistakes when students read aloud, but it is the capability to move through text easily, to make meanings and respond to what the author is saying without struggling too much over the letters and sounds or the individual words. Fluent readers self-monitor their meanings and know "fix-up strategies" to use when they get confused. Figure 2.4 lists behaviors that are related to this phase of literacy development. Teachers can use these descriptors as flexible benchmarks for what they expect to see young readers and writers do as they move past emergent-reading behaviors. Some first graders and many second and third graders can be expected to develop these literacy behaviors.

Behaviors Demonstrating that a Learner Is Developing Fluent Meaning-Making

Frame 1: *Self Efficacy*

- Is willing to work at meaning-making
- Is developing stamina for reading and writing for longer periods of time
- Is developing independence in reading and writing tasks
- Attaining confidence in reading and writing but may be self-conscious about sharing and accepting opinions of others

Frame 2: *World Knowledge*

- Is more able to construct meaning using prior knowledge
- Copes with greater variety of vocabulary, syntax, genres, styles
- Understands that life experiences as well as other book experiences influence construction of meaning

Frame 3: *Literacy Knowledge and Strategies*

- Begins to read word for word fluently with familiar texts
- Uses strategies to help with unfamiliar words, such as looking at pictures, beginning and ending letters
- Writes phonetically with most of the sounds in a word represented, with vowels the last to be represented
- Can read own writing after time has elapsed
- Others can read writing
- Begins to use all cueing systems in reading
- Separates words with spaces when writing
- Is becoming more conscious of and uses conventions of writing
- Has a repertoire of conventionally spelled words
- Phonetic spelling becomes more and more conventional
- Begins to be aware of sequence and uses some elaboration in writing
- Length of writing increases
- Begins to read silently
- Silent reading becomes more comfortable and efficient
- Uses knowledge of story structure to aid in prediction
- Beginning to understand different text structures and reads them differently
- Begins to use writing for a variety of different purposes
- Willing to revise writing when prompted, usually at word level
- Reads for pleasure

Frame 4: *Reflection*

- Talks differently about nonfiction than narratives

Continued . . .

Figure 2.4 Behaviors demonstrating fluent meaning-making.

> - Becoming more able to explain book choices
> - Is able to talk about writing topics
>
> **Frame 5: *Functional and Critical Literacy***
> - Is learning that he/she does not have to agree with what is written
> - Is learning about point of view and fact and opinion
> - Becoming aware of audience and the need to accommodate readers

Figure 2.4 (*Continued*)   Behaviors demonstrating fluent meaning-making.

Finding Reasons to Read and Write

What does this mean for you and your colleagues as you work to help the students you are worried about? It means that all children need a rich and stimulating environment to support their literacy development—no matter what previous literacy experiences they bring and no matter what their current expertise. Too often in schools we provide these rich environments for the students who are moving along as expected, but we put the children who are not progressing very quickly through tests to identify their weaknesses and (lovingly) drill them on the very skills they can't do very well. If we break the literacy process into skills to be practiced and sight words to be memorized, we actually make it harder for these children to make sense at all. We often end up convincing these children that they can't be readers. And sometimes they never become readers, no matter how systematically and thoroughly we remediate them. There certainly is a time and place for explicit instruction focusing on particular elements of reading and writing, but only in the larger context of authentic literacy—messages in books, newspapers, magazines, and in the children's own writing. If all children are to become joyfully and independently literate, it must happen in a context they see as both fun and functional.

As you are building a rich literacy and literature environment for your young children, to help them grow up reading and writing, think about it from their point of view. Are they reading for you, just to make you happy, just to get a sticker on their paper? Or do they really see that reading and writing can help them do things they need and want to do? Of course, there are times in each school day when that may not be possible; but, for the most part, students should be reading and writing because they need and want to communicate with each other, with authors, and with audiences outside the classroom. We used to think of this kind of activity as "enrichment" or "extensions," to be done after the skill sheets were finished. Now we know that these experiences can and should be the heart of a rich classroom literacy environment. This kind of environment would include daily reading, daily writing, and daily opportunities to talk about how we read and write.

Daily Reading

Children cannot learn to read confidently and fluently if they are not spending lots of time reading. One of the first questions to ask when you think about your classroom and how it supports emergent literacy development is this, "How much are these children actually reading each day?" Sometimes, when we take the time to actually count the minutes students are expected to be reading books, magazines, textbooks, and messages displayed on the walls, we realize that they really spend most of their day listening to us give instructions, moving from place to place, getting out materials or putting them away, or talking with their classmates. Research, logic, and experience tell us that sustained silent reading is a critical part of each school day. (Although it is not always "silent" in the classrooms where children are just learning to read!)

This daily reading would also include opportunities to hear good literature read aloud. Trelease (1995) and others have convinced us of the power of the read aloud for building background knowledge and vocabulary, for exposure to important concepts and works of literature, and for the pure pleasure of hearing wonderful language. Childrens (and adults) of all ages benefit from daily read alouds.

Table 2.2 shows a reading chart to list all the kinds of reading that happens in your room. You might even estimate the number of minutes students spend doing each kind of reading each day. What if you invited students to chart it for themselves for a few days?

Table 2.2 Daily reading chart.

Type of Reading	Whole Group Read Alouds	Whole Group	Small Group	Pairs of Students	Alone	Alone with teacher
Picture Storybook						
"Stuff" on the walls						
Poetry						
Informational Books						
Textbooks						
Computer						
Newspaper & Magazines						
Worksheets & Handouts						
Student-Authored Books						
Messages to One Another						
Other?						

Daily Writing

The same is true of writing. Kids who write a lot learn to write better and better. Many teachers and researchers have pointed out that you can read without writing, but you can't write without reading. It is during the writing process—as young children try to decide which letter and which word to write to represent their message—that many children learn about letters and sounds and punctuation. Writing also helps us take an active stance toward literacy. It is our experience that children who know they are authors read more actively than children who don't have a clear understanding about how books come to be written. Frank Smith (1982) says it best when he talks about the functions of writing:

> Writing is for stories to be read, books to be published, poems to be recited, plays to be acted, songs to be sung, newspapers to be shared, letters to be mailed, jokes to be told, notes to be passed, cards to be sent, cartons to be labelled, instructions to be followed, designs to be made, recipes to be cooked, messages to be exchanged, programs to be organized, excursions to be planned, catalogs to be compared, entertainment guides to be consulted, memos to be circulated, announcements to be posted, bills to be collected, posters to be displayed, cribs to be hidden, and diaries to be concealed. Writing is for ideas, action, reflection, and experience. It is not for having your ignorance exposed, your sensitivity destroyed, or your ability assessed (p. 211, 1982).

Talking about Reading and Writing

The heart of our job as literacy teachers is to learn to talk to our students about how reading and writing work. It is most helpful if we can have those conversations "at the point of need." As a child is trying to make sense of the silent "e" at the end of "lake," we can remind him of how his best friend's name is spelled, "JAKE." In conversations like that, at just the right time, a young reader can learn more in a couple of minutes than he might have learned from hours with flash cards and worksheets. Clay (1998) writes about "teaching as conversation," as she emphasizes the importance of knowing where kids are and what they need next so that we can talk to them about what they are just about to learn.

This kind of talk about reading and writing can happen with the whole group, as we are doing Shared Reading or as teachers "think aloud" as they demonstrate how they read and write. An overhead projector can be a great tool for that kind of demonstration. Teaching conversations are probably more helpful, however, in small group settings or one-with-one. In small groups, it's more likely that all the students will be tuned in to the conversation, and the teacher can more easily pay attention and respond to nonverbal cues and to students' questions. Guided reading, which we talk about in chapter 8, is an excellent context for these small group conversations about strategies-in-use. Teacher conferences are powerful contexts for these conversations. Try to plan some one-on-one time with each child at least once every couple of weeks, when other students are busy at centers or with independent reading.

One of our goals is for children to talk about their own decisions as they read and write. When a child can talk about her strategies (and show you that she has not just memorized what she has heard the teacher say), we know that she has control over her literacy strategies. That's when we know she is off to a wonderful start and quickly moving forward as a reader and writer.

Questions for Further Dialogue

We hope that reading this chapter has prompted you to think about some of the questions and puzzling issues you see as you try to find what each of your students needs. Here are some discussion starters for you and your colleagues to think about:

- In Table 2.3, we have outlined the contents of chapters 3–9 about the kids whose literacy development puzzles us. As you look at that chart and make choices about which of the chapters you want to read first, think about these questions: Which of your students is really puzzling you right now? What is she or he doing that is so unexpected? How have you tried to support her or him? What seems to "work?"

Thinking About Support for Young Readers and Writers 23

Table 2.3 Instructional suggestions for eight emergent readers and writers who puzzle us.

	Rich Language & Literature Environments	Assessment	Literacy Engagements/Instruction	Literacy Centers
Chapter 3 Tiffany Kids Who Just Sit and Watch	Authentic Purposes for Literacy Daily Reading Teacher Read Alouds Daily Writing Daily Talk about Reading and Writing	• Drawing • DL-TA Assessment	• Real Audiences and Authentic Tasks • Story Telling • Play Acting • Assisted Reading • Directed Reading-Thinking Activity	• Play-Like Center • Magic Glasses Center
Chapter 4 Buddy Kids Who Don't Seem to Care	Authentic Purposes for Literacy Daily Reading Teacher Read Alouds Daily Writing Daily Talk about Reading and Writing	• Getting Acquainted • Parent/Guardian Questions • Retelling	• Student Inquiry • K-W-L Chart • Peer Groups for Reading and Writing • Think Aloud	• Classroom Travel Agency • Pet Hospital
Chapter 5 Kevin Kids Who Don't Understand How Written Language Works	Authentic Purposes for Literacy Daily Reading Teacher Read Alouds Daily Writing Daily Talk about Reading and Writing	• Phonemic Awareness • The Book Handling Knowledge Task • Environmental Print Awareness	• Shared Reading • Key Words • Language Experience Approach • Phonemic Awareness Instruction • Guided Writing • Interactive Writing	• Alphabet Center • Pocket Chart Center
Chapter 6 André Kids Who Are Reluctant to Write	Authentic Purposes for Literacy Daily Reading Teacher Read Alouds Daily Writing Daily Talk about Reading and Writing	• Dictation • Student Writing • Interest Inventory	• Real Audiences and Authentic Tasks • Teacher Demonstrations • Brainstorming • Text for Wordless Picture Books • Shared Writing • Routines for Writing Fluency	• Fast Writing Center • Recorder/Reporter Center
Chapter 7 Allen Kids Who Don't Get the Big Picture When They Read	Authentic Purposes for Literacy Daily Reading Teacher Read Alouds Daily Writing Daily Talk about Reading and Writing	• Retellings • Reflective Interviews	• Rich Book Introductions • Re-Enactments • Response Activities • Sketch & Guess • Readers' Theater • Conceptual Maps	• The Writing Center • The Discovery Center

Continued . . .

Table 2.3 (*Continued*) Instructional suggestions for eight emergent readers and writers who puzzle us.

	Rich Language & Literature Environments	Assessment	Literacy Engagements/Instruction	Literacy Centers
Chapter 8 Shaniqua Kids Who Don't Use Visual and Structure Cues to Make Meaning	Authentic Purposes for Literacy Daily Reading Teacher Read Alouds Daily Writing Daily Talk about Reading and Writing	• Modified Miscue Analysis • Student Reflection	• Choosing Appropriate Books • Guided Reading • Guided Writing (one-on-one) • Cloze Activities	• Book Center • Word Study Center
Chapter 9 Matt Kids Who Know About Letters and Sounds and Still Can't Read	Authentic Purposes for Literacy Daily Reading Teacher Read Alouds Daily Writing Daily Talk about Reading and Writing	• Teacher Observation • Conferencing • Diagnostic Spelling Test	• Ownership, Authenticity, and Authorship • Conversations about Language and Literacy • Interactive Writing • Assisted & Repeated Readings	• Dialogue Journal Center • Listening Center
Chapter 10 Rosa Kids Who Have Little Experience with "School English"	Authentic Purposes for Literacy Daily Reading Teacher Read Alouds Daily Writing Daily Talk about Reading and Writing	• Strategy Interview	• Rich Oral Language and Literacy Opportunities • Choral Reading • Drawing • Video & Multi-media • Mind-mapping	• Environmental Print • Big Book Center • Art Center

- When you say something "works" what do you mean?
- How much time do your students spend reading and writing? When they are not actually engaged in reading and writing, what are they doing? Can you capture more reading and writing time for them?
- How much do you actually know about your children's literacy experiences at home? How do you know? Have you visited their neighborhoods and homes? Have you asked their parents?
- Is it appropriate to encourage your children to read and write at home if that is not a part of their home culture? If so, how do you encourage students to read and write at home?

Resources for Further Inquiry

Avery, C. (1993). . . .*And with a light touch: Learning about reading, writing, and teaching with first graders.* Portsmouth, NH: Heinemann.

Bissex, G. (1984). *Gnys at work: A child learns to read and write.* Cambridge, MA: Harvard University Press.

Burns, M. S., Griffin, P., & Snow, C. E., (Eds.) (1998). *Starting out right: A guide to promoting children's reading success.* Committee on the Prevention of Reading Difficulties in Young Children. Washington, DC: National Academy Press.

Clay, M. (1998). *By different paths to common outcomes.* York, ME: Stenhouse Publishers.

Fisher, B. (1991). *Joyful learning: A whole language kindergarten.* Portsmouth, NH: Heinemann.

Fisher, B. (1996). *Inside the classroom: Teaching kindergarten and first grade.* Portsmouth, NH: Heinemann.

Goodman, K. (1996). *On reading.* Portsmouth, NH: Heinemann.

Goodman, Y., & Burke, C. (1980). *Reading strategies: Focus on comprehension.* New York: Holt, Rinehart & Winston.

Mallow, F., & Patterson, L. (1999). *Framing literacy: Teaching/learning in K–8 classrooms.* Norwood, MA: Christopher-Gordon.

Teale, W. (1986). Home background and young children's literacy development. In W. Teale & E. Sulzby (Eds.), *Emergent literacy: Writing and reading* (pp. 173–206). Norwood, NJ: Ablex Publishing Corporation .

Teale, W., & Sulzby, E. (1989). Emergent literacy: New perspectives. In Dorothy Strickland and Lesley Morrow (Eds.), *Emerging literacy: Young children learn to read and write.* Newark, DE: International Reading Association.

Trelease, J. (1995). *The read-aloud handbook.* 4th Ed. New York: Penguin Books.

Wells, G. (1981). *Learning through interaction: The study of language development.* Cambridge, UK: Cambridge University Press.

Chapter 3

Kids Who Just Sit and Watch

Tiffany waits quietly for the teacher to tell her what to do. A reluctant writer and a passive reader, Tiffany refuses to step out of her comfort zone and take risks. When reading with the teacher or a peer, she stares at the page and waits for someone else to help when she gets stuck. If she reads an unfamiliar word, she says it softly, with a questioning tone. When she uses her one (inefficient) strategy, sounding out, she sometimes produces nonsense words. Rather than self-correcting, she just continues reading. She seems to have no real interest in the literacy process and seems to see no purpose for reading and writing in her own life. When writing, her focus is on using words she knows because she wants to spell everything correctly. Her writing is almost exclusively patterned writing about things she likes, such as "I like my dog", "I like my cat," or things that she knows, such as the color or the size of objects. She writes no narratives because she says she "doesn't know what to write about." She often sits for long periods of time just thinking, without writing a word. She does not like to share her writing and never uses the classroom mailbox to send her friends or the teacher a message.

What Is Happening?

As Tiffany's teacher tells the other members of the campus Literacy Team about Tiffany, they are able to come to a consensus around some statements that seem to summarize the critical aspects of Tiffany's literacy:

- Tiffany does not seem to understand that she can use reading and writing to get things done.
- Tiffany will not take risks to make guesses in her reading or in her writing.
- Tiffany's reluctance to engage in reading and writing is keeping her from the experiences that would help her learn more.

So What Does This Mean?

The teachers use these questions to explore what prompts Tiffany to do these things and what the teacher might try as she invites Tiffany to venture into more authentic literacy engagements:

- What are some of Tiffany's interests (maybe unrelated to school and literacy)?
- What does Tiffany know about that no one else in the class does? How can she become the class expert on that topic?
- Who is important to Tiffany? How might literacy become an integral part of that relationship?
- When does Tiffany seem to open up and talk more? How can we build on those conversations as language experiences?
- What does Tiffany think good readers and writers do as they look at books and as they write stories?
- What can Tiffany say about what she does when she's reading and gets stuck?

Now What Shall We Do?

The Literacy Team first suggests that Tiffany's teacher try to dig deeper, to learn more about Tiffany's reluctance to participate. Later, they brainstorm for suggestions about literacy engagements or instructional experiences that might build on Tiffany's strengths and encourage her to be less passive. Next, they talk about literacy center activities for Tiffany, and they end their discussion with suggestions for home support that would be especially helpful for her.

Learning More About Tiffany

Drawing

When you ask her to draw about what she understands, does she convey more information through her drawings than she can through writing? Will she take risks when she draws that she does not dare when she writes? Here are some suggestions

- Draw a picture of where the story takes place, including as many details as you can imagine.
- Draw a cartoon strip representing the sequence of events in the story.
- Draw a "snapshot" of your favorite part of the story.

DL-TA Assessment

Directed Listening-Thinking Activity (DL-TA) provides opportunities to assess and develop critical listening and thinking skills. After dividing the text into appropriate segments that can be single paragraphs or several pages, depending on the content, the teacher reads the text aloud to the student(s). At the appropriate stopping places in the text, the teacher asks questions that

- Activate thought . . .   What do you think?
- Agitate thought . . .   Why do you think so?
- Require evidence . . .   How can you prove it?

Students are asked to predict and then use the text to confirm or disconfirm their predictions. Using DL-TA supports the reader who does not want to take risks, while allowing the teacher to observe the thought processes of students, or lack thereof. DL-TA should give you some insight into what Tiffany is thinking as she listens to a story. This strategy is an adaptation of Stauffer's (1975) Directed Reading-Thinking Activity (DR-TA). Of course, retelling what she hears is always a good opportunity to show what she understands. It might be less intimidating if she can retell a story with a partner.

Literacy Engagements for Tiffany

Real Audiences and Authentic Tasks

One way to begin to engage Tiffany is to offer her the opportunities to read and write to and for real people with real purposes. These opportunities could include a pen pal in another grade, a reading buddy in kindergarten to read aloud to, an adult mentor at school who would be willing to listen and talk about reading and writing with Tiffany. This mentor would not be a tutor, but rather someone who would share purposes and experiences with literacy, who would encourage Tiffany in literacy activities for real audiences.

Storytelling

Storytelling is another way to engage children like Tiffany. Telling stories gives a child experience in organizing thoughts, sequencing events, and participating actively that might not ordinarily occur in the daily classroom activities. Round robin storytelling is a safe way to begin. The teacher starts the story with a sentence or two and each person in the group adds a sentence. You can begin with a familiar story and after practice with the technique, new stories can be made up on the spot. When you first begin doing this activity, the stories may wander or lack structure, but continued work on the technique leads to better and better stories. Of course, your reading aloud of good literature builds a repertoire in the students' minds.

Storytelling can also be accomplished with wordless picture books that contain a story line. Using the pictures as the guide, the story can be made up on the spot with a small group. This can be a teacher-directed or independent small group activity, with a performance before the whole group occurring later after practice. Storytelling can also be accomplished using props, puppets, or story characters and objects on a flannel board. You can ask the librarian of the nearest public library to come and tell a story to the class. You can even have the children ask their parents or grandparents about family stories that might be appropriate for telling at school. This involvement of the whole family personalizes literacy as no other technique can do.

Play Acting

Play acting or drama is a way to involve and bring students together in ways that promote attending to both verbal and nonverbal communication. Drama in the classroom encourages creative thinking and problem solving and individual learning responses. Since a variety of responses could be considered "correct" in dramatic situations, children can feel secure in taking risks. Students can pantomime actions while a story is being read aloud. Again using wordless picture books, students can act out what is pictured, using only actions. Another way to incorporate drama in the classroom uses the teacher as the narrator of a story while students use hand puppets for the speaking roles with simple dialogue and actions. If you want to involve the whole class in drama, you can have several groups working on reenactments of various stories, fables, myths, or folklore. Students can make simple paper plate masks taped to popsicle sticks to enhance the telling of familiar stories. Watch how the repetitive language of familiar stories creeps into the reenactments that the children do! These reenactments can be very simple requiring only a short time of preparation, or could involve the students in script writing and rehearsals. Either way, active involvement, comprehension, and repeated oral reading are the keys to success. Be sure to ask parents, other classes, and community members to view the performance so the students have an authentic audience.

Assisted Reading

Tiffany could also benefit from having a trained tutor work with her as often as possible. The tutor, who could be a parent, a retired teacher who lives in the neighborhood, an older excellent reader in the school, or a high school student who gets out of school early, could provide the opportunity for Tiffany to read easy, predictable books repeatedly. These repeated readings would boost Tiffany's fluency and confidence. A box of books on Tiffany's level could be provided, and the tutor could be taught to do assisted reading and repeated reading with Tiffany. Tiffany needs many demonstrations by fluent readers and writers for many purposes.

Probably the most supportive of strategies is assisted reading. It is a technique for increasing fluency in which a child reads along with the teacher as the teacher reads orally. It is best done with a predictable text and is most often used with emergent readers or older readers who are experiencing difficulty. Using fluent oral reading as a vehicle, the ultimate goal of assisted reading is fluent silent reading. Follow these steps

- Choose an appropriate text, preferably one that the child has heard or read before.
- If it is an unfamiliar text—read the story to the child, sitting side-by-side so that the child's attention is directed to the print as the story is being read, then read it together.
- If the text is familiar, invite the child to read along with you as you read fluently but at a slightly slower pace than you would normally read.
- Point to the text as you read.
- Do not stop for mistakes made by the child. Keep going.
- Read the entire text before stopping for questions, discussion, word study, and so forth.

Assisted reading is best accomplished when the text is shared, the teacher's voice is directed toward the student and the teacher or student points to the print. Poetry is also an excellent vehicle for assisted reading.

DR-TA

Another simple, yet powerful, instructional strategy that helps students like Tiffany is the Directed Reading-Thinking Activity, or DR-TA. Using this strategy consistently improves comprehension and promotes active reading and critical thinking by having students predict, read, question, and prove or disprove their prediction. It can be used as a strategy with an individual, small or large group, narrative or expository texts. Sometimes a child who does not get the big picture when reading a story, but likes factual material, will have an easier time with nonfiction reading.

During planning, the teacher divides the text into appropriate segments which can be single paragraphs or several pages, depending on the content. Direct student's attention to the title, pictures, text structure, headings, graphs, and so forth. Following this, ask questions that

- Activate thought . . .   What do you think?
- Agitate thought . . .   Why do you think so?
- Require evidence . . . How can you prove it?

The student reads the segment of the text silently to confirm predictions and, during discussion, the text is used to confirm or disconfirm predictions. Students are expected to use the context to figure out vocabulary which may be new or difficult. This vocabulary can be discussed using predictive questions such as: What do you think this word means? Why do you think so? The process is repeated until each segment of the text has been read.

Literacy Center Activities for Tiffany

The "Play Like" Center

This center can be a different focus every few weeks. It can be set up as a grocery store, a restaurant, a catalog order center, or a toy store. Supplies might include empty food boxes and cans, menus from various restaurants (especially familiar ones in the area), catalogs and magazines, toys, pencils, notepads, restaurant order pads, sale flyers from grocery stores, play money, a roll of cash register tape, a play cash register, a phone book and play phone, and plastic food items. The children can "play like" they are shopping by making a list, placing orders for food, ordering from a catalog, buying toys at the toy store, looking for names in the phone book and writing phone numbers. Each time the center is changed, explicit demonstrations need to be given, although as you know, most children have a lot of experience at "playing like" what they see their parents do. This real life literacy center pulls kids into the adult situations where literacy is used to get things accomplished.

"Magic Glasses" Center

This center is an easy one to prepare—two pairs of "magic eye glasses" and a pointer. Pairs of children don the glasses and take the pointer in hand. They walk around the room, reading all the print on the walls—bulletin boards, charts, posters, word walls, labels, name charts, student work, book bindings, and so forth. In this buddy reading situation, children can support one another and use their emerging reading strategies to "decode" the room!

Home Support for Tiffany

Tiffany's parents need to be encouraged to involve Tiffany in their everyday activities that involve literacy, such as grocery lists, reading the newspaper, charts of chores, and thank you letters. She needs to be included in family conversations, encouraged to give opinions, urged to take risks in problem-solving at home.

Resources for Further Inquiry

Mallow, F., & Patterson, L. (1999). *Framing literacy: Teaching/learning in K–8 classrooms.* Norwood, MA: Christopher-Gordon.

Rhodes, L., & Dudley-Marling, C. (1988, 1996). *Readers and writers with a difference.* Portsmouth, NH: Heinemann.

Richards, M. (2000). Be a good detective: Solve the case of oral reading fluency. *The Reading Teacher, 53,* 534–539.

Stauffer, R. (1975). *Directing the reading-thinking process.* New York: Harper & Row.

Weaver, C. (1994). *Reading process and practice.* Portsmouth, NH: Heinemann.

Chapter 4

Kids Who Don't Seem to Care

Buddy strolls into his second-grade classroom the first day of school with his shoulders cocked back and a scowl on his face that seems to say, "You can't make me!" He appears disinterested when his teacher asks him to choose a book that he would like to read. He does choose a book and takes his seat but immediately begins bothering the students around him. Later, when everyone is writing, he makes paper airplanes because he can't think of anything to write about despite several efforts by the teacher, suggesting topics and asking questions about what he did over the weekend.

After several days, his teacher conferences with him to find out about his interests. Reluctantly, in monosyllables, Buddy answers questions, saying a few words about his home in the country, his animals and finally, with animation and far more details, his love of rodeo events. His family has recently moved to the city from a ranch in Arizona, where his uncle was helping him learn to rope calves. He tells his teacher that he will be a world champion roper, that he doesn't believe that rodeo cowboys need to read and write, and that he hates school.

What Is Happening?

Buddy's teacher takes this information to the Literacy Team and they help her formulate these statements about Buddy's literacy:
- Reading and writing are not easy for Buddy, and he tends to avoid participating in classroom literacy activities.
- Buddy has a great deal of experience and knowledge about raising and showing animals and about rodeos.
- Buddy responds well when faced with tasks and challenges that seem "real" to him, like rodeos and calf roping.
- Buddy works hard, even at things that are difficult for him, when he sees a purpose.

So What Does This Mean?

As the teachers talk about Buddy, they seem to focus on these questions as productive avenues to pursue:

- Does Buddy have the chance to make choices about what he reads and writes at school?
- Do classroom activities provide an opportunity for Buddy to explore his interests?
- Does Buddy have a chance to use reading and writing as tools for activities he sees as important or significant?
- Are there areas where Buddy can become the "class expert?"
- Do the classroom resources (books, magazines, the Internet) offer materials to support Buddy's areas of interest?
- When Buddy actually engages in reading and writing in the classroom, what are his areas of strength in terms of literacy knowledge and strategies? Maybe he acts as if he doesn't care because he doesn't have the strategies he needs to make sense when he reads and writes.
- How can we encourage Buddy to move beyond familiar topics and genre, to stretch and enhance his literacy experiences beyond his current comfort zones?
- How can we be sure that Buddy continues participating in the classroom community, contributing his special knowledge and beginning to learn from others?

Now What Shall We Do?

The Literacy Team first suggests that Buddy's teacher use a range of assessments to learn more about Buddy's literacy strategies. Later, they brainstorm for suggestions about literacy engagements or instructional experiences that might build on his strengths and encourage him to be more enthusiastic. Next, they talk about related literacy center activities that Buddy might do independently and then make suggestions for home support.

Learning More About Buddy

Getting Acquainted

All teachers have their favorite ways they get to know their students at the beginning of the year. Here are some ideas we have found helpful:

- Me Museum (table or bulletin board on which one student at a time displays photographs, objects, books, and explanations about his or her personal life)
- Autobiographies (timelines, mind maps, stories, books or any other format that gives students opportunities to tell stories about their lives)
- Author's Chair and Publishing (multiple opportunities to write, revise, illustrate, and share stories and inquiries with audiences)
- Class Yearbook (ongoing collections of writing, photographs, and artifacts that tell the unfolding story of this particular learning community)
- Dialogue Journals and Written Conversations (opportunities for students to respond to the teacher and one another).

Parent/Guardian Questions

Depending on your situation, you could use these questions in a telephone or face-to-face interview. You might develop a questionnaire for adults to complete (or for adults and children to complete together) (see Figure 4.1). The important point is to make sure the students, their families, and you become partners as you come to know one another.

Literacy in Our House

1. What kinds of things does our family read and write at home?

    (Circle the ones that you use often.)

Books	Church materials	Catalogs
Newspapers	Scrapbooks	Bus schedules
Magazines	Shopping lists	Menus
Letters	E-mail and Internet	Bills & checks
Recipes	Manuals	Advertisements
Other _____		

2. How does your child spend his or her free time?

3. What are your child's typical activities after school? on the weekends? during school holidays?

4. How would you like to see your child's reading or writing improve?

Figure 4.1 Literacy in Our House.

Retelling

To this point, we have assumed that Buddy isn't engaging in reading and writing because he doesn't see that it is important or interesting. We can't ignore the possibility, however, that Buddy doesn't seem to care because he simply can't read or write very well. Sometimes it is difficult for teachers to tell the difference between "won't" and "can't." In order to establish Buddy's comprehension levels, retellings can be very helpful.

In a retelling, after hearing or reading a message—narrative or expository—a student is asked to tell everything she remembers from the passage. A retelling should include main ideas and details, in the same sequence as the original message. It is different from a summary, which includes only the essential information, leaving out elaboration and details.

Retellings can be written or oral, free or structured. In a free retelling, the teacher simply asks the reader to tell everything he remembers from the message, and the student proceeds without prompting. For a structured retelling, the teacher can ask the student to use an outline, a graphic organizer, or a series of pictures or other concrete representation designed to help trigger the retelling.

Obviously, a retelling demonstrates whether the reader understands and remembers the main ideas and the details of the passage. In addition, a retelling should also reflect the text structure of the original message. For example, a student's retelling of a story can suggest whether or not she understands that stories have a setting, characters, problems, and resolution. Or a retelling can indicate whether a learner understands that expository text can be an argument with a logical structure, with a particular sequence, and a particular relation between a conclusion and its supporting evidence. For these reasons, retellings provide a more useful assessment of comprehension than a list of comprehension questions. Follow these steps

- Choose a whole passage, either narrative or expository, that has a clear text structure.
- Ask students (either in groups or individually) to read the passage, either orally or silently. To assess listening comprehension, read the passage to the student(s). Tell them that when they have finished reading they will be asked to tell everything they remember from the passage.
- Give them ample time for reading and thinking about the passage.
- Decide whether you will let them go back to the text during the retelling. Your decision will depend on your purpose. If you are simply trying to assess reading and comprehension, going back to the text will not interfere. If you are trying to assess retention or memory of the text, then have them close the book prior to the retelling. If you are using the retelling results to document growth over time, remember to use the same procedures for each administration to make comparisons possible.
- Ask them to retell everything they remember. Decide whether you want an oral or written retelling. If written, do you want to encourage them to use drawings to accompany the text?
- When using retellings as an instructional strategy, lead the students in discussions about what makes a good retelling.

Table 4.1 is an example of a rubric you can use to evaluate retellings and to spot possible teaching points.

Table 4.1 Retelling rubric.

	None	To a low degree	To a moderate degree	To a high degree
Repeats information directly stated in the text				
Includes the gist of the text				
Includes inferences based on information in the text				
Includes generalizations about the main problem or theme or thesis				
Attempts to connect reader's background knowledge with the text				
Attempts to apply generalizations based on the text to real world situations				
Includes affective or emotional responses to the text				
Organizes the retelling coherently				
Demonstrates as sense of audience				
Demonstrates control of the conventions of oral or written language				

Literacy Engagements for Buddy
Student Inquiry

There are no recipes or formulas for classroom inquiry. Leading students in successful inquiry comes from the teacher's sincere effort to connect with students' interests and areas of strength and a strong commitment to authentic learning and literacy. What are you and the students interested in? What do you need to know? What needs to be done in your school? In your community? What resources do you have? Frances tells the following story about an inquiry she led in her Kindergarten class.

> One balmy spring afternoon, several weeks before the end of school, my kindergarten children and I took off on a walk around the neighborhood. These walks had become a regular outing; and after we got back to school, they became a literacy event as we wrote and talked about what we had seen and done on the walk. I had my camera with me and I was going to take pictures of each child so that they could give them to their mothers for Mothers Day.
>
> We had become acquainted with several people in the neighborhood and I was hoping that we could use one particularly beautiful yard for the pictures. Flowers of all colors were blooming in the flower beds. The elderly lady was working in the yard when we arrived and was glad to see us, as we had visited her and her beautiful yard several times before. She allowed the children to pick some flowers and we took our pictures.
>
> While I had been preoccupied with picture-taking, the kids had roamed all over the yard and two boys had made an interesting discovery in the side yard. There were hundreds of snails in the flower bed and they ran to tell the rest of us about their find. The snails had big shells, with brown and tan stripes. What a treasure! With a twinkle in her eye, the lady very willingly let us haul all the snails we could find back to school. We had probably 50 snails, carried in shirt tails and skirt "baskets." Now what would we do with them?
>
> Immediately upon getting back to school, we put them on a table to see what they would do. After a few minutes, they began to emerge from their shells. The children and I watched with fascination as 50 snails began to glide all over the table, leaving shiny, slimy trails. This source of wonder became our unit of study for the next week.
>
> First, we scoured the school for several boxes and then went outside to collect plants, rocks, and soil to make habitats. We put water in jar lids, arranged the plants, rocks, and soil and put in the snails. Then we headed to the library for books about snails. I read informational books to the children, we wrote a language experience story about our walk and about the snails, we drew pictures, and the children wrote about snails. They wrote snail stories and factual little books. One mother snail even laid eggs, as if the event were planned just for our benefit. The habitats with the snails were a source of endless fascination for over a week, when some of the snails began to die. So, we took the live ones outside and let them go and buried the dead ones. We had learned so much. . . . I had learned how to capture the moment, how to use the moment to enhance the literacy learning that took place in the classroom, had modeled the inquiry process, and guided the inquiry of inquisitive 5 and 6 year olds. And the kids had learned about using informational books, had added words to their vocabulary, had written about what they were learning about, had given short talks to other classes about the snails.

This is the kind of authentic inquiry that we hope to invite our students to do. If this kind of open-ended teaching is new to you, you may be more comfortable at first with some routines or instructional frames that organize inquiry for us. Here is one:

K-W-L Chart

K-W-L is an instructional strategy for guided reading of expository text by activating prior knowledge, setting purposes for reading, encouraging active reading, monitoring comprehension, and holding readers accountable for gaining information from the text by helping formulate questions to be answered by reading (Ogle, 1986; Carr & Ogle, 1987). This strategy provides a flexible structure for teachers who are just beginning to invite their students to do inquiry. Here is a brief description of how to do it:

K-W-L		
What I know (K)	What I want to find out (W)	What did I learn? What do I still want to know? (L)

Figure 4.2 K-W-L Chart.

1. Use individual K-W-L sheets or a large piece of paper divided into three columns, that can be seen by the entire class. Label the columns
   - What I Know (K)
   - What I Want to Know (W)
   - What I Learned (L)
2. Brainstorm, listing everything that is known about the topic to be read under the "What I Know" column K.
3. With teacher guidance, students generate questions by skimming title and subtopics of the text, looking at the pictures and boldface words, and discussing the text. Questions are recorded in the "What I Want to Know" column W.
4. Students read text, stopping periodically to record what they have learned in the last column labeled "What I Learned (L)." If the student encounters words they do not understand, they record their questions in the middle column. The W and L columns can be revised continuously.
5. Together with the teacher, summary statements are written in the L column, checking to confirm answers to questions in the W column.

Peer Groups for Reading and Writing

Buddy would also probably benefit from reading and writing in small groups with students who are enthusiastic. He could work in groups to do the inquiry activities mentioned above or to complete K-W-L charts. Collaborative learning experiences in social studies and science might help him be more enthusiastic and engaged in his reading and writing. Buddy reading is also a productive way to let students work with others who can support them in a variety of ways. Some teachers let students pair up to do their independent reading, but sometimes a teacher might want to assign buddies for a particular reading or writing activity. Also, look for opportunities to pair Buddy with younger or less experienced readers. After practicing his reading of a particular book, he could read it to and with a younger child. Those kinds of social settings for reading and writing can be motivating for students like Buddy.

Think Aloud

The think aloud, as an instructional strategy, gives students an opportunity to develop thinking about their reading strategies. This is done by modeling how a good reader thinks through what is being read, stops at intervals, thinks about how the text is being understood, and uses self-talk about the strategies that are being used. Thinking aloud gives verbal expression to what goes on in the mind when reading and what needs to be done in the form of fix-up strategies when comprehension breaks down—such as, self-questioning and knowing how to find answers; retelling in order to understand; predicting, reading, and verifying; rereading and reading on; and inferring.

Here is a brief description of how to conduct a think-aloud:

- Explain the process of what is happening in a reader's brain during reading-sampling cues, making predictions, stopping and asking if the reading makes sense and if it sounds right.
- Reading from the beginning of a new story, model the process of alternately reading aloud, predicting and verifying, questioning, rereading and/or reading on for a more complete understanding, and demonstrating your thinking process as you infer from the text, identifying the strategies that are being used. The students should have a copy of the text and be reading along.

- Prompt students to think aloud by asking questions such as: "What do you think?" "What clue in the text gave you that idea?" "Why do you think that?"
- Have students read the next section with teacher supervision, thinking aloud and talking about strategies. Gradually turn over the responsibility to the students.
- Gradually build a class list of strategies that good readers use as they read for meaning, and practicing these through think alouds.

Literacy Center Activities for Buddy

Classroom Travel Agency

Maps, brochures, Internet sites, travel logs, post cards, atlases, and almanacs are just a few of the resources that can support a "travel agency" in your classroom. You may want to introduce the learning center in connection with social studies. Your class can work together to plan a pretend trip to sites you are studying. As students learn to use the resources independently, they can dream up their own projects.

Pet Hospital

Ann Rousse, who teaches pre-kindergarten classes in Alief, I.S.D., decided that one way to encourage her students to learn how to ask good questions was to set up a "pet hospital" as a play center. She stocked it with clipboards and forms from her local veterinarian's office, with stuffed animals, and medical supplies. The students were soon interviewing one another about their animals' aches and pains. They enjoyed learning about inquiry in this setting; and with Ann talking about questions and inquiry during other activities, she is convinced they are asking better questions in other settings as well.

Home Support for Buddy

Buddy's family is already supporting him as a learner, but they may not see opportunities for connecting his interests to literacy learning. Helping them see these connections would be a great beginning. Sending home books about his interests and suggesting that the family talk about movies and television programs together would be another way to support Buddy's literacy learning. If the family has access to the Internet at home or at a neighborhood library, that would be a wonderful resource for Buddy to pursue his personal inquiries.

Resources for Further Inquiry

Carr, E., & Ogle, D. (1987). K-W-L plus: A strategy for comprehension and summarization. *Journal of Reading, 30* (7), 626–631.

Duncan, D., & Lockhart, L. (2000). *I-search, you search, we all learn to research: A how-to-do-it manual for teaching elementary school students to solve information problems.* New York: Neal-Schuman Publishers.

Ogle, D. (1986). K-W-L: A teaching model that develops active reading of expository text. *The Reading Teacher, 39* (6), 564–570.

Short, K., Harste, J., with Burke, C. (1995). *Creating classrooms for authors and inquirers.* Portsmouth, NH: Heinemann.

Chapter 5

Kids Who Don't Know How Written Language Works

Kevin entered first grade after two years in a private school. Although he had been taught the names and sounds of the letters and could sing the alphabet song, he showed little evidence of knowing or being able to use the alphabetic principle. In his journal, he drew pictures and occasionally wrote his name, but often forgot the names of the letters. The drawings in his journal were elaborate and during sharing time, he told stories about his drawings. Occasionally he would use the letters in his name to signify meaning. At times he would copy print that he saw in the room; but when asked about it during a teacher conference, he didn't know what he had written. Even when the teacher wrote for him, he paid little attention to what was being written and could not read it back. When he was in the reading center, he held a book and "read" the pictures and was able to sketchily retell the story. He seemed to enjoy looking at picture books on his own, but did not attempt to read unfamiliar text. He identified some books by the pictures on the front and knew the sequence of familiar stories. When asked, he would respond that he could not read.

What is Happening?

When Kevin's teacher took this story to her Literacy Team, she had already summarized what she knew about him in this way:

- Although he has had a great deal of instruction about letters and sounds, Kevin has trouble recognizing and using letters in books or in his own writing.
- Kevin does not seem to understand the alphabetic principle, and he doesn't seem to know letter sounds.
- Related to that, Kevin does not use invented spelling.

- Kevin knows that pictures can signify meanings, and he uses drawings to tell stories to his classmates.
- Kevin seems to know that he is not reading conventionally.

So What Does This Mean?

In talking about Kevin, these are the questions that the Literacy Team used to reflect on Kevin's strengths and his targets for growth:

- Does Kevin know that reading and writing are supposed to make sense?
- Can Kevin understand and respond to stories and informational text when it is read aloud? Can he make predictions and inferences as he is listening?
- Is Kevin a good problem-solver in other areas of his life—on the soccer field? playing computer games?
- Can Kevin find patterns in math class? Is he able to recognize numerals?
- What are some topics that Kevin knows about and is interested in? How can we build on his prior knowledge?
- Does Kevin watch classmates using letters, sounds, and so forth, as he participates in shared reading and writing?
- Can Kevin hear and talk about sounds in oral language?
- What about Kevin's oral language? Does he participate in conversations with his classmates? With adults? Is his oral language conventional in terms of syntax? Is his vocabulary knowledge typical for his age and grade?
- What can Kevin's parents tell us about how he engages in oral and written language opportunities at home?

Now What Shall We Do?

The Literacy Team first suggests ways for Kevin's teacher to learn more about him. Later, they brainstorm for suggestions about literacy engagements or instructional experiences that might build on his strengths. Next, they talk about possible literacy center activities and suggestions for home support.

Learning More About Kevin

This description focuses on what Kevin apparently does not know about letters and sounds in reading and writing. It is important to find out more about what he does know. Are there any contexts (for example, computer games) where Kevin is beginning to use the alphabet or other symbols to make sense? And can Kevin begin paying attention to how letters and sounds are used as he participates in shared reading? In interactive writing? What is Kevin's knowledge about the world—what prior knowledge and interests can we use to build on?

Phonemic Awareness Assessments

When you see a child for whom letters and sounds are not making sense, it may help to know whether he can hear sounds in oral language. Can he separate sounds in words? Can he put them together again? Can he play rhyming games? Can he recognize alliteration? Here are some phonemic awareness assessments that teachers might use (Griffith & Olson,1992). These are listed in order of difficulty:

- Is the child able to hear rhyming words? Select ten pairs of words, in which at least five pair rhyme, for example, hill, pill. Explain that rhyming words end the same, and give a few examples. Pronounce each pair, asking the child if they rhyme.
- Is the child able to add another rhyming word to a group of three rhyming words? Select five groups of three words that rhyme and ask the child to tell you another real word or made-up word that rhymes with the other three, for example, hop, stop, mop.
- Is the child able to blend speech sounds into words? Select ten words with two phonemes, for example, ate. Select ten words with three or four phonemes, for example, can. Divide five words into rimes and onsets, such as /c/ -an, and divide the other five words completely, such as /th/ /i/ /s/. Pronounce the segmented words, asking the child to guess the complete word.
- Is the child able to isolate speech sounds? Select nine, three-phoneme words, for example, cake. Explain that you will ask for the beginning sound in three words, for example, goat; the middle sound in three words, for example, tape; and the end sound in three words, for example, book.
- Is the child able to completely segment all the sounds in words?
- Is the child able to remove phonemes and say how the word is changed? Select five words that can have the initial sound removed and still be a word, for example, tape. For an example, say the word and say the word without the /t/ (pronounce letter sound, not letter name)—tape, ape. Say the five words, asking the child to say the word and the word without the initial phoneme. Select five words that can have the final sound removed and still be a word, for example, main. For an example, say the word and say the word without the /n/ (pronounce the letter sound, not the letter name)—main, may. Say the five words, asking the child to say the word and the word without the final phoneme.

Of course, in addition to being aware of phonemes, children need to know much, much more about the way oral and written language works. Phonemic awareness is probably much more important for children who are in classes where a great deal of time is spent on explicit phonics instruction than in classrooms where most of the children's time is spent reading and writing books and other messages. Logic tells us that phonemic awareness can help children make sense of phonics instruction, as the teacher focuses on how letters and sounds make words.

Yopp-Singer Phonemic Awareness Test

The Yopp-Singer Test of Phoneme Segmentation assesses a child's ability to articulate the separate sounds of a spoken word in order. This instrument can help teachers determine which children need more activities that facilitate phonemic awareness. The test is given individually and takes 5–10 minutes per child. The following directions are given

> Today we're going to play a word game. I'm going to say a word and I want you to break the word apart. You are going to tell me each sound in the word in order. For example, if I say "old," you should say "/o/-/l/-/d/" (Say the sounds, not the letters.) Let's try a few words together.

The practice items are *ride, go,* and *man.* Help the child with each sample, segmenting the sounds if necessary and encouraging the child to repeat the phonemes. Ask the child to do the same on the test, which has 22 items. Give feedback such as "That's right," or provide the correct response if given an incorrect response. Write the incorrect responses so that you can do an analysis.

Children who segment all or nearly all correctly are considered phonemically aware. Those who segment some correctly are considered emergent, while those who segment only a few or none correctly lack appropriate levels of awareness. These are the children who will need the benefit of phonemic awareness activities.

Because of the increased political and public attention to phonemic awareness, this test and others like it are currently in wide use. Teachers we work with, however, have found that many young children have great difficulty with the Yopp-Singer Phonemic Awareness Test. Some children lose interest quickly; some do not understand the instructions after repeated explanations; and some even walk away, refusing to engage in what seems to be a meaningless task. As with any assessment procedure, decide whether this is going to be useful and then watch students carefully to see whether the information you are getting is representative of what they demonstrate in other contexts.

Yopp-Singer Test of Phoneme Segmentation

Student's name _____ Date _____

Score (number correct) _____

Directions: Today we're going to play a word game. I'm going to say a word and I want you to break the word apart. You are going to tell me each sound in the word in the order you hear it. For example, if I say "old," you should say "/o/-/l/-/d/." (*Administrator: Be sure to say the sounds, not the letters, in the word.*) Let's try a few together.

Practice items (*Assist the child in segmenting these items as necessary.*):
          ride   go   man

Test items: (*Circle those items that the student correctly segments; incorrect responses may be recorded on the blank line following the item.*)

1.	dog _____		12.	lay _____
2.	keep _____		13.	race _____
3.	fine _____		14.	zoo _____
4.	no _____		15.	three _____
5.	she _____		16.	job _____
6.	wave _____		17.	in _____
7.	grew _____		18.	ice _____
8.	that _____		19.	at _____
9.	red _____		20.	top _____
10.	me _____		21.	by _____
11.	sat _____		22.	do _____

The author, Hallie Kay Yopp, California State University, Fullerton, grants permission for this test to be reproduced. The author acknowledges the contribution of the late Harry Singer to the development of this test.

Figure 5.1   Yopp-Singer Phonemic Awareness Test.

The Book Handling Knowledge Task

Adapted from Clay (1993) and Goodman, Altwerger and Marek (1989), this is a way to document what the child knows about the characteristics of books and how text works. This is an individual assessment used with emergent readers that gives the teacher clear and concrete knowledge about a child's understandings and metalinguistic ability to explain and talk about what he/she knows about books and the print in books. With the information gleaned from this assessment, the teacher can then fill in gaps or clarify misconceptions through demonstrations.

Here's how it works. The teacher and child sit side by side with a suitable picture storybook. Select a book that has a title page with the title and author's name; clear, bold print; and pictures on every page with only a line or two of fairly large print. If possible, videotape the interview. If this is not possible, record the responses in writing. Conduct the interview in a conversational and game-like manner, responding enthusiastically to the responses of the child. Table 5.1 provides specific procedures, taken from *Framing Literacy: Teaching/Learning, K–8* (Mallow and Patterson, 1999):

Table 5.1 The Book Handling Knowledge Task.

Item	The teacher does . . .	The teacher says . . .	The child may respond . . .
1.	Show book; sweep hand under title.	"What's this called?"	"Book" "Storybook" "Story" Name of book
2.	Display book.	"What do you do with it?"	"Read it" "Look at it" "Open it"
3.	Display book.	"What's inside it?"	"Story" "Pictures" "Words" "Letters" "Things"
4.	Present book wrong way up and backwards to child.	"Show me the front of the book and open it so that we can read it together."	Any indication of front or first page.
5.	Take the book and turn to page in book.	Hold on to page and say," "Show me a page in the book. Is this a page?	Point to page, "Yes"
6.	Give the book to child.	"Please read this to me."	Record all responses. Child may talk about the pictures. Child may play at "reading." Child may refuse to read.
7.	Hold the book so child can see.	"I'll read the story to you. Show me where to start reading."	Indicates print on page.
8.	Turn to the next page.	"Show me the top of the page." "Show me the bottom of the page."	Indicates top. Indicates bottom.
9.	Show the page to the child.	"Show me with your finger where I have to begin reading."	Points to first line on page.
10.	Show the page to the child.	"Show me with your finger which way I go as I read this page."	Left to right on the page.
11.	Continue to show page.	"Where then?"	Top to bottom.

Continued . . .

Table 5.1 (*Continued*) The Handling Knowledge Task.

Item	The teacher does...	The teacher says...	The child may respond...
12.	Slowly read the page.	"You point to the story while I read it."	Print/voice match, close match.
13.	Display page.	"Where do I go now?"	Turns page or points to print on next page; left to right order.
14.	Read the next two pages. If possible, turn to a page with picture and print on it and turn book upside down.	"Can you or I read this now? Why or why not?"	Turns book right side up. Says that its upside down. "Turn it up."
15.	Show child how to use two index cards to view aspects of print. Use as curtains over a window, framing letters as appropriate.	"Let's put some of the story in this window. I want you to close the curtains until I can see just one letter... two letters."	Shows one letter. Shows two letters.
16.	Open "curtains."	"Now use the curtains to show me one word... two words."	Shows one word. Shows two words.
17.	Open "curtains."	"Show me the first letter in a word."	Points to first letter.
18.	Remove cards.	"Show me a capital letter—any capital letter."	Points to a capital letter.
19.	Read to middle of story.	"Show me where I am."	Points to print on page.
20.	Read to end of story. Close book and pass to child.	"Show me the name of the book" or "Name the story."	Points to cover or title page.
21.	Explore comprehension.	"Tell me something about story."	Record all responses.
22.	Give the book to the child.	"Show me the beginning of the story." "Show me the end of the story."	Opens book to first page, points to first line. Turns to last page, points to last line.
23.	Point to title page.	"It says here (read title of book) by... (read author's name). What does by... (say author's name) mean?"	"He wrote it." "She made up story." "She made the book."

Environmental Print Awareness Inventory

This is a hands-on series of tasks in which a young child is asked to identify common products used in the home in forms that provide less and less contextual information. The child is asked to identify first the product in the actual package; then the actual logo cut from the box or package; next, a black and white copy of the logo; and finally, the typed product name.

The purpose of assessing a young child's environmental print awareness is to find out the extent to which he/she interprets print in the environment and the degree of appropriateness of the child's responses. By analyzing the responses to the tasks, the teacher will be able to note the cues or significant features that the child uses to make responses and the language the child uses to talk about components of written language.

Gather actual packages, boxes, cans, or sacks of common household products that would be found in almost any home and would be known by a young child such as toothpaste, bath soap, cereal, band-aids, fruit or soft drinks, tissues, candy, and so forth. Have a variety and use 6 to 8 for the assessment. Put these in a box or large zip-lock bag.

Gather another identical set of products and cut the graphics or logos with the name of the product from the box or sack. Mount these cutouts on tagboard and store in a plastic sleeve. Photocopy these logos or graphics, mount on tagboard, and store in a plastic sleeve.

These same logos or graphics are then typed in large print on index cards, using lower case and capital letters. Store in a zip-lock bag along with index cards of other print commonly seen in the child's environment such as Wal-Mart, STOP, Dairy Queen, McDonald's, Texaco, or the neighborhood grocery store.

Rather than taking notes during the assessment, use a tape recorder to record the child's responses and keep the atmosphere casual, game-like and conversational. As you take out each product, graphic from the package, copy, and printed index card to show to the child, ask these questions:

- What do you think this says?
- How do you know that?
- Show me what you are looking at.
- What does that tell you?
- Does that tell you something special?

Present the items of each level of difficulty at least several days apart and change the order of the items each session. Note the child's responses:

What does the child do (such as pointing at a feature)?
- Print
- Pictures
- Symbols and designs
- Colors
- Size or shape of package

What does the child say (verbal reference to feature)?
- Print
- Pictures
- Symbols and/or designs
- Colors
- Personal experience (I eat this at breakfast)
- Ego-involved responses (Because I thought it, like it)

Also, you can note the appropriateness of the child's responses:
- Exact response ("Coca Cola" or "Coke")
- Related concept ("cereal" for "Cheerios" or "coffee" for "Sweet and Low")
- Appropriate function ("Wash dishes" for "Ivory Liquid")
- Linguistic response ("You're so funny, rabbit" for "Trix cereal")
- Print specific response ("M" for "M&M's")
- Chaining response ("Vitamins" for "Tic-Tacs")
- Inappropriate response ("Can I have one?" for "Hershey's Kiss")

Here are some questions to ask yourself to help the analysis:
- Is the child able to demonstrate the use of context to "read" a product name?
- Does the child point to a letter or letters and name them? Or associate letters with his/her name?
- Is the child able to draw on knowledge and experience from other contexts?
- Does the child make connections to construct knowledge?
- Does the child become restless, bored, or listless when asked to read the less contextualized logos? What does that tell you?

This assessment is adapted from one developed by Yetta Goodman (1986).

Table 5.2 Environmental Print Checklist

Environmental Print Checklist					
Name: _____ Age: _____					
Setting: _____ Date: _____					
Product Names	**Product**	**Logo**	**Copy**	**Hand-Printed**	
KEY FOR ANSWERS				
A: Appropriate function	L: Linguistic response			
C: Chaining response	N: Nonverbal response			
E: Exact response	P: Print-specific response			
I: Inappropriate response	R: Related concept			

Literacy Engagements for Kevin

Shared Reading

Shared Reading is one way to help young readers and writers learn more about how written language works. Many early reading teachers have used it for a long time with Big Books or language charts that make it easy for all the students to read a common text. Shared reading embodies the four phases of Holdaway's (1979) natural learning model:

- Demonstration (teacher reads)
- Guided participation (children participate in re-reading)
- Individual practice (independent re-reading)
- Performance (child volunteers to read aloud)

Shared Reading emphasizes the fact that reading can be a social experience with a Big Book that has enlarged print that the children can see, follow, and read simultaneously as a group. It was based on procedures observed during bedtime story time in the home, and it is most successful when the text is predictable. That means that there are repeated patterns in the letters and the sounds of the words, in the phrases, and in the story structure. Predictable text also uses concepts and sequences that are familiar to children. Eric Carle's *The Very Hungry Caterpillar* (1979) is predictable because of the repeated language pattern, the sing-songy rhythm, the sequence of days of the week and numbers, and because the objects and images are familiar to most children.

Here is a brief description of how you can do it with your students:

1. Children are gathered comfortably on the floor, teacher sitting in a chair beside an easel displaying the enlarged reading material.
2. Group re-reads favorite rhymes, poems, songs, or stories while the teacher points to the print.
3. At least once a week, a new book is introduced by talking about the author, looking at the pictures, and predicting what the story will be about, relating the ideas to children's lives.
4. The teacher reads the story with zest and enjoyment, discusses the story, and reads it again, pointing to each word and inviting children to chime in when they can.
5. During further re-readings on subsequent days, the teacher may pause before key words or mask words or parts of words to focus attention on the print.
6. Re-reading can be done independently by individual or small groups of children as the story becomes more and more familiar.
7. Children learn through incidental and direct teaching regarding conventions of print; strategies such as predicting, self-correcting, and reading for meaning; sight vocabulary; letter-sound relationships; and voice-print match.

Key Words

First described by Sylvia Ashton-Warner (1963) in her book, *Teacher,* the concept of key words was developed to elicit what she called "organic" vocabulary from rural Maori children that she taught in New Zealand. These were words that were powerfully engaging for the children. Ask the child to tell you his "important words," maybe just one each day, and write them on index cards. Let the student watch you write the word(s). Have the child trace the words, copy them, put them into dictated or written stories, match them, play games with them, act them out, or sort them. Daily, spend a few moments with each child reviewing these personal word banks.

Language Experience Approach (LEA)

Language Experience Approach uses the child's own language and provides a natural way to build concepts of print and beginning reading processes through the generation of text (Van Allen, 1976). In a language experience lesson, the connection is made between the spoken and written forms of language. This approach encourages memory for text and is highly predictable because it is the child's language. To accomplish this, informally discuss a book, a shared experience, something the child has done or something that has happened to him. Through questioning and discussion, sequence ideas, then act as scribe as the child dictates ideas. As you write with colored marker on chart paper, remarking on the features of print that you use, the child's attention is directed to the writing and both teacher and child say words as they are written. After dictation, use a pointer as you re-read the text directing attention to left-to-right progression, sound-symbol correspondence, sight words, and print conventions. LEA can be done with an individual child, a small group, or a whole class.

The dictated story can be typed, copied, and taken home for illustrating and reading practice. Sentences from the dictation can be written on sentence strips that the children manipulate to match the original order and they can also be used in the pocket chart center (discussed later in this chapter). Language experience dictations can be summaries of stories, learning logs, original stories, steps in a process, lists of items, a letter, or observations. Using this approach, you are demonstrating many of the uses of language.

Phonemic Awareness

Assessment and development of phonemic awareness should take place within the context of daily meaningful literacy activities. Activities that require children to perform tasks with words they have heard in the daily read aloud or shared reading can be made into games that are played as a whole group or in small groups under teacher direction.

Choose books, rhymes, poems, chants, songs and games that lend themselves to word play. Literature that allows children to play with language such as books with alliteration, assonance (the repetition of vowel sounds within words), and rhyming should be read to the students daily.

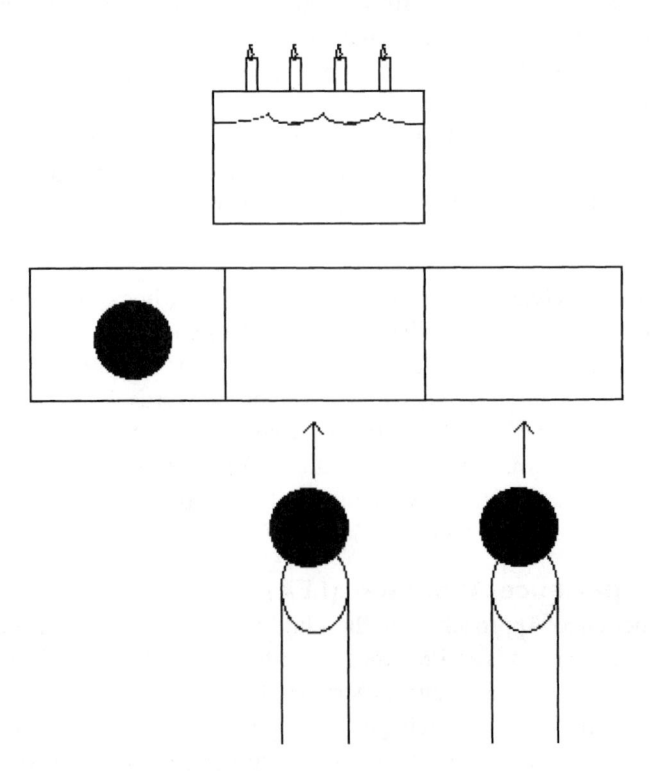

Figure 5.2 Elkonin boxes.

Explicit instruction in hearing sounds in words can be facilitated with the use of Elkonin boxes for practice in hearing sounds and boxes for writing letters, both of which are used in Reading Recovery (Clay, 1993). A matrix should be drawn that contains a box for each phoneme (not letter) in the word. For example, "cat" would need three boxes, "show" would need two boxes. As the teacher slowly pronounces the word, she moves colored discs into each box, sound by sound. Gradually the child takes over the task of moving the disks.

Boxes can also be used for hearing sounds and writing letters. Draw a box for each sound in a word the child wants to write. For example, tree would need two boxes, Jim would need three boxes, ship would need three boxes, and so forth.

Tr	ee

J	i	m

Sh	i	p

Both of these activities should be within the context of enjoying stories and using literacy for real purposes. These activities can be helpful in problem-solving in unfamiliar words in both reading and writing. We should always be careful that children see these activities as tools for reading and writing, not as ends in themselves.

Literacy Centers for Kevin

Alphabet Center

The Alphabet Center is a permanent center set up for independent practice of the word work, phonics principle, and/or spelling of the day. The center contains small tubs of plastic magnetic letters in both upper and lower case, word cards, and picture cards, ABC books, and a cookie sheet or dry erase board. In this center, children manipulate the magnetic letters in order to better understand the alphabet sequence and letter/sound relationships. Beginning letters can be matched to pictures; upper and lower case letters can be matched; familiar words can be spelled. If colored markers are added, the students may write a word after manipulating the plastic letters to form the word. The activities vary according to what has been taught that day and must be clearly understood by the students.

Pocket Chart Center

The Pocket Chart Center can be coordinated with shared reading, a familiar read aloud, or a nursery rhyme that has been read and chorally chanted. The sentences or lines from the book or poem are copied on sentence strips. Working collaboratively, a small group of students puts the sentences from the book or lines from the poem in the pocket chart in the correct order. Some sentence strips can be cut apart, and each individual word is put in the pocket chart in sequence to form a sentence.

Home Support for Kevin

Parents need to be encouraged to read to Kevin, pointing to the print, asking him to join in after repeated readings. Environmental print needs to be pointed out to him. Conversations about letters and words will raise his awareness. Parents could write notes to him and provide paper and pencils for experimentation with writing. Use charts for chores, allow him to help with grocery lists and shopping—pointing out names of products, names of letters and sounds.

Resources for Further Inquiry

Ashton-Warner, S. (1963). *Teacher.* New York: Simon & Schuster.

Carle, Eric. (1979). *The very hungry caterpillar.* New York: Collins Publishers.

Clay, M. (1993). *The early detection of reading difficulties* (3rd ed.). Auckland, NZ: Heinemann

Goodman, Y. (1980). The roots of literacy. In M. Douglass (Ed.), *Claremont reading conference, 44th yearbook* (pp. 1–32). Claremont, CA: Center for Developmental Studies.

Goodman, Y. (1986). Children coming to know literacy. In W. Teale & E. Sulzby (Eds.), *Emergent literacy: Writing and reading* (pp. 1–14). Norwood, NJ: Ablex Publishing Corporation.

Goodman, Y., Altwerger, B., & Marek, A. (1989). *Print awareness in pre-school children.* Program in Language and Literacy, Arizona Center for Research & Development. Tucson University of Arizona.

Griffith, P., & Olson, M. (1992). Phonemic awareness helps beginning readers break the code. *The Reading Teacher, 45* (7), 516–523.

Holdaway, D. (1979). *The foundations of literacy.* Sydney, Australia: Ashton Scholastic.

Ketch, A. (1991). *The delicious alphabet in Great Britain.* In K. Goodman, L. Bird, & Y. Goodman (Eds.), *The whole language catalog* (p. 39). Santa Rosa, CA: American School Publishers.

Yopp, H. (1992). Developing phonemic awareness in young children. *The Reading Teacher, 45* (9), 696–703.

Yopp, H. (1992). Read-aloud books for developing phonemic awareness: An annotated bibliography. *The Reading Teacher, 48* (6), 538–542.

Yopp, H. (1995). A test for assessing phonemic awareness in young children. *The Reading Teacher, 49* (1), 20–29.

Chapter 6

Kids Who Are Reluctant to Write

André seems to be deep in thought. Although the rest of the class has been writing for half an hour, André has produced nothing. He has spent fruitless time searching his messy desk for a piece of clean paper, and finally a friend who sat next to him gave him some. Now he sits over that blank piece of paper. The children around him talk as they write and share ideas with each other, but André sits silent. Even the teacher's conversations, conferences, and quiet encouragement do not seem to help André put anything on the paper. When asked what he would like to write about, he answers with an "I don't know." He does not respond to story starters but fills in blanks when the class does pattern writing, especially if another child thinks of a word to put in the blank. Even copying is so laborious for André that he begins but seldom finishes what he wants to copy. Although he sometimes responds to what other children write, he seldom comes up with ideas of his own. When at rare times he offers an idea, he produces a minimal line or two of writing that contains incomplete thoughts written in large handwriting, nonconventional spelling, all capital letters, and no punctuation.

What Is Happening?

André's teacher and her colleagues on the Literacy Team have no trouble identifying the issues they need to talk about to find some way to help André.

- André has a difficult time engaging in independent writing.
- He seems not to realize that he does have important things to say.
- He shows little awareness of relationship between reading and writing.
- He may not understand basic print concepts related to the alphabet, placement of writing on the page, and punctuation.

So What Does This Mean?

André's teacher and her colleagues generate these questions as they try to understand how to support him:

- Does André understand that oral language can be written down and read?
- Does André understand how print works?
- Does André understand sound-symbol relationships enough to write his thoughts down? In what ways does he use invented spellings to represent a written message?
- What meanings does André get from environmental print? What characteristics of environmental print does he pay attention to?
- How much experience does André have in supported reading and writing situations so that he can gradually build his independence?
- How can we find ways to show André that writing and reading can be fun and functional?

Now What Shall We Do?

The Literacy Team and André's teacher talked about a range of assessments that would give them more information about André's literacy strategies. They also brainstorm for suggestions about literacy engagements or instructional experiences that might encourage him to be more eager to write. Next, they talk about related literacy center activities that he might do independently and make suggestions for home support so that André can begin seeing that writing is fun and useful.

Learning More About André

Dictation

André may be reluctant to write because he does not understand how to do it. He may have to struggle so much to decide what letters to use that he avoids writing at all. Dictation is one way to find out what he knows about how written language works. Dictation is a fairly straightforward process. After reading a story, help your student write a letter to his family about it. Together you decide what you want to say. Let him write it, with as little help from you as possible. See whether he can write sentences that you are saying to him. What does he seem to know and what can he do? What seems to trip him up? What questions does he ask? What kind of support can you give him?

Student Writing

Once André begins writing more, we can watch his writing for clues about what he knows and what he still needs to learn about how written language works. He can keep a learning log as he explores topics of interest. He can make lists of what he knows and what he still needs to learn. Of course, he can write and illustrate books to present what he has learned to his classmates and to audiences outside the classroom. As André works in the Literacy Centers, he may generate more writing than he does in his individual writing assignments.

Interest Inventory

It is much more likely that André will begin writing if he is writing about topics of personal interest and significance to people he knows. Sometimes a brief interest inventory can help teachers identify and record what students' interests are. Look for engaging ways to ask children for this information. For example, what about having them draw about their interests? How about having them interview one another, asking a few questions and reporting the answers to the rest of the class?

---

1. What do you like to do after school, in your leisure or play time?

2. What hobbies or collections do you have?

3. What places has your family visited recently?

4. What are your favorite television shows? songs? movies? books? games? school subjects?

5. Do you have a library card? How often do you go to the library?

6. Do you have any books at home? What are your favorites?

7. What do you like to read about? Who are your favorite authors? What are your favorite kinds of books?

8. Does your family get magazines or newspapers at home? How often? What are some of the magazines?

Figure 6.1 Interest Inventory Questionnaire.

Literacy Engagements for André

Real Audiences and Authentic Tasks

With a child who is reluctant to write, it is sometimes difficult to tell whether he does not know how to do it or he simply chooses not to. He may not see a significant reason to write. It is certainly easier to teach students how to write if they are writing something that is important to them. For that reason, look for real audiences and real reasons to write. Notes and letters, signs to post around the room, and books to author for the classroom library are just a few examples. Other ideas will come from your daily activities.

Teacher Demonstrations

Nothing is quite so powerful as a teacher demonstrating her own struggles and successes and strategies as a writer. This can best be accomplished with a whole class by using the overhead projector. Your own thinking about your writing is made visible as you talk your way through the writing you are doing on the transparency. As the children see you generate ideas, write, scratch out, add words, worry out loud, and move words around, they realize that all writers go through similar processes.

Brainstorming

Brainstorming can be used for many purposes; but in this case, it provides a way for André to generate ideas for writing and to pick a topic. As a teacher demonstration, this again provides the students a window into the teacher's thoughts and shows them how they can do it for themselves. For example, on chart paper or overhead projector, you might list the topics:

- Buying a new car
- Planting a garden
- Our new puppy
- When I sprained my ankle

Deciding to write about when you sprained your ankle, demonstrate how you would brainstorm any or all of the possible subtopics you could include in this story:

- How it happened
- Where it happened
- What it felt like
- Going to the emergency room
- Learning to walk on crutches

This brainstormed list of subtopics can serve to narrow the focus of your writing, or can be the outline from which you write.

Writing Text for Wordless Picture Books

This is a strategy which builds on the child's oral language and storytelling facility and uses teacher demonstration to support the emergent reader and writer. Since the text is constructed by the child by reading the pictures and using his own language, it is highly predictable. This strategy is excellent for promoting fluency with repeated re-readings.

Here is a brief explanation of how to do it:

1. Introduce the wordless picture book by reading the title and allowing the child to look at the entire book, talking about the picture and the author's message.
2. Invite the child to tell the story by looking at the pictures again.

3. Using a pad of 3 x 5 Post-its, invite the child to dictate the story page by page as you write the text of each page on the Post-it and apply it to the page.
4. Read the book repeatedly.
5. Pull the Post-its off pages, put them on the table in random order, have the child apply them to the correct pages, and read each page.

This strategy can be done with an individual or a small group. With a group, the text can be transcribed on large chart paper while the learners dictate. Then the teacher can read aloud, using a pointer to track the text. As appropriate, the teacher can use echo reading (teacher reads a line and the learner repeats), assisted reading (learner reads with the teacher), or choral reading (teacher and learner read together by arranging text for differing voices in a variety of ways).

Individual small books can be made of that message, with room for each learner to illustrate. Students can choose words from the story to be written on index cards. The child can keep those words in a zip lock bag and scatter them out each day for reading and combining. These can be taken home to share and read aloud.

Shared Writing

Shared writing is not a substitute for independent writing; but, when used judiciously, it can support students who are having trouble getting started. Shared writing combines teacher and student input with teacher demonstration. The students and teacher collaborate to create a text. The teacher does the writing on a chart or transparency while the whole group or small group contributes ideas to the text. This writing could be based on the shared reading of the week, the daily news, a shared experience such as a field trip or video, a summary of content learned that week, retelling of a story, or text for a wordless picture book. This is very similar to the Language Experience Approach that has long been used with emergent readers and writers. LEA emphasizes the meaning-making process, creating a message to be read and re-read. Shared writing, however, emphasizes sound/symbol correspondence, writing conventions, story structure, spelling, or audience. Shared writing seems to have become a preferred context for explicit instruction about these aspects of written language. As we said earlier, it should not be the only writing experience for emergent readers and writers. Children should have a range of opportunities to write and draw their ideas for many different audiences, and they should have opportunities to use invented spellings as they are exploring written language and how it works.

Routines for Writing Fluency

Of course, emergent writers focus more on composing a message and representing that message through drawings and words. As they mature in their use of written language, children will be more conscious of print conventions—spelling, punctuation, and handwriting. At that point, we can begin focusing on editing as a separate step in the process. For reluctant writers like André, however, it is critical to focus on first draft writing as they build fluency.

In first draft writing the purpose is to get thoughts on paper and, then revise later, when it's time to share the message with an audience. The best way to accomplish writing fluency is through regular opportunities for first draft writing. The students may then choose from these first draft pieces a few to carry through the entire writing process to publication. As we observe children engaged in the writing process, we teach specific skills as they are needed for clarity, organization, elaboration, sequencing, and so forth.

The sharing of these writing pieces with an audience provides a purpose for the student.

To encourage student authors, teachers need to make sure they provide at least five things in their instructional plans:

- Extended time to write about topics of the students' choice
- A range of purposes and real audiences for whom to write
- Honest response and feedback from peers and from the teacher
- Real audiences who can and will respond to the authors' work
- Multiple and varied demonstrations of effective writing

As student authors complete their first drafts, teachers can use a range of instructional methods to assist them in revision, editing, and publishing their work for real audiences. Fluency, however, develops as students are encouraged to write daily about a range of topics, in a range of genres.

Writing Roulette This is an activity that can be used in various ways to encourage first draft writing. For many students, it becomes a game—an enjoyable way to build writing fluency. Follow these steps

- Have students get into groups of three or four.
- Have students begin writing a story or memory of their choice.
- Have students write for five minutes. When time is called, they should finish the sentence and stop, even if that thought is incomplete.
- Have students pass their papers to the students on their right.
- All students read the "new" paper and begin writing where the first writer was interrupted. There should be no conversations between the writers. They should write for four minutes.
- Repeat the process, giving each person three minutes to add to each story, until the paper is passed back to the original writer.
- That student is to read the paper and write a closing paragraph.
- Within each group, the original writers can read their papers aloud to the group.
- Each group may choose one piece to share with the large group.

This strategy creates lots of laughter when each original writer sees how different the final paper is when compared to his beginning.

Written Conversations. (See also dialogue journal center in chapter 9.) Written conversations are just that—a chance for two or more people to write their messages to one another. This is an excellent strategy to use with reluctant writers because the challenge is just to write one question or comment, not an entire message. With very reluctant writers, we have made it an "I Spy" game, so that each participant can make guesses about the secret object, rather than generate a conversation. Here are some general guidelines:

- Two writers (can include the teacher) sit down to communicate in writing without the use of oral language.
- The topic may be provided (content recently taught or a classroom issue). This strategy may be used to begin the day with a morning conversation using prompts such as, "What did you do for fun yesterday?" "What did you learn yesterday?" "How do you feel about . . . ?"
- The writing continues until the topic has been covered or until time is called.
- The writers are not allowed to talk during this activity, unless there is a need to clarify spelling or word meaning.

With emergent writers, it may be helpful to combine pictures and words.

Fast and Furious Writing   This is yet another strategy to build writing fluency, particularly among reluctant writers. A prompt is provided or generated by the class. Typical prompts for young children would be favorite (or least favorite) food, pets, games, and so forth. Students are instructed to write without stopping for five to ten minutes. They are to write anything that comes to mind without being concerned about spelling or mechanics. This is similar to a brainstorming activity except everything is written without conversation. The writing may then be shared with small or large groups. If this is done daily or weekly, students can keep track of how many words they can generate in a given time period. Although this kind of "race" will soon be less interesting than writing meaningful messages, we have discovered that reluctant writers can be engaged in this activity in which they are competing against their own best times.

Pen Pal Letters/School Post Office   This is yet another attempt to provide a real audience to encourage students to increase their writing fluency. It can also be a great motivator for reluctant writers. Have students choose a pen pal within the classroom or school. A neighboring school or community might also be a source of pen pals. If your classroom computer is connected to the Internet, check out the many pen pal opportunities available on-line. For this to be successful, sending and receiving letters should become a predictable part of the classroom routine. Develop a postal service within the school or classroom that will be operated by the students who have participated in the pen pal letter exchange. This activity will encourage even the most reluctant writer to write!

Journal Writing   Of course, journals can serve many purposes in addition to the development of writing fluency. Many teachers use reading response journals and learning logs that connect to content objectives. Personal journals help children connect writing to their own lives. We recommend that, if journals are truly going to encourage writing fluency, the topics be generated by the class or by individuals. Occasionally, a teacher may suggest a topic related to common readings or an important event, but student choice is a critical ingredient of the effective journal.

Lucy Calkins (1990) uses the term "writer's notebook" rather than journal, emphasizing that this is a place to extend our individual thinking—our discoveries, our questions, and our wonderings—that it should be available at all times of the day (and night) so that students can record their thoughts immediately. Calkins also emphasizes the importance of reading and re-reading the notebooks, to look for important discoveries or insights that can trigger further writing and learning. In this way, the notebook becomes a valuable prewriting resource as the student keeps a list of possible topics, memories, favorite phrases and words, and names of books for possible ways to say things.

Here are a few general guidelines for journal writing:
- All students are provided time to write freely on a topic of their choice in a personal diary or journal.
- The time should be scheduled so that the students expect to write on a consistent basis. It should be student choice as to when and with whom they choose to share their entries.
- Teachers may read and respond to selected journal entries, and students should be held accountable (and graded) for writing in the journal, but not on the content or the quality of the writing. This is first draft writing!

Literacy Centers for André

Fast Writing Center
The fast writing center has dry erase boards and markers, erasers, and a timer. Set the timer for five minutes (or two or three minutes, depending on students' experience and needs) and have the students write as much as they can during that time. A display chart for students to record the number of words they write helps with record keeping.

Recorder/Reporter Center
The recorder/reporter center has a clipboard with paper and a pencil. This center is designed for two children to walk around the room with the clipboard and pencil. The reporter is to talk quietly about the activities and the learning that is taking place while the recorder writes it. After the children are well oriented to this activity, they can be allowed to go to other classrooms to observe the learning and record it. You might want to tell the teachers when to expect your recorder and reporter. These observations can then be shared with the class.

Home Support for André

André's parents can be encouraged to use dialogue journals to write and receive notes about daily activities, lunch money, trips to Wal-Mart. They can ask family members to write letters to André, and make a game of answering those letters. Weekly newsletters to parents from the teacher help keep parents informed about class activities and provide suggestions for simple follow-up activities for home. Use children's names in the newsletter and encourage parents to read and re-read them with their child.

Resources for Further Inquiry

Button, K., Johnson, M., & Furgerson, P. (1996). Interactive writing in a primary classroom. *The Reading Teacher, 49*, 446–454.

Calkins, L. (1990). *Living between the lines.* Portsmouth, NH: Heinemann.

Calkins, L. (1994). *The art of teaching writing.* Portsmouth, NH: Heinemann.

Carbo, M. (1978). Teaching reading with talking books. *The Reading Teacher, 32*, 267–273.

Cunningham, P., & Allington, R. (1999). *Classrooms that work: They can all read and write.* New York: Harper Collins.

Routman, R. (1991). *Invitations.* Portsmouth, NH: Heinemann.

Rhodes, L., & Dudley-Marling, C. (1988). *Readers and writers with a difference.* Portsmouth, NH: Heinemann.

Chapter 7

Kids Who Don't Get the Big Picture When They Read

Allen sits alone with his teacher during her planning period. Perplexed with his lack of comprehension of most, if not all, of what he reads, she knows she needs to work one-to-one with him in order to understand what he is doing. Although she had listened to him read and knew that he was a fairly accurate oral reader of books on his level, he typically gave random answers to questions that were asked and contributed little to class discussions about their readings.

The teacher has selected a new storybook from the library that she was sure was not familiar to him and on a level that she felt he could read. She tells Allen that she wants to listen to him read the new book and get his opinion of it. He shrugs his shoulders, opens the book, and begins reading on the first page, with hardly a glance at the title or the pictures in the book. As he reads the book, word for word, he rarely self-corrects, even when what he says makes no sense. He does not use the pictures for clues to words, and does not at any point stop and talk about what he is reading. When Allen finishes reading, his teacher asks him to tell her everything he remembers from the story. She then asks questions that build on his retelling. His retelling is brief, and he can answer few of her questions. He clearly doesn't know where to look for the answers.

What Is Happening?

In the Literacy Team meeting, the teachers quickly focus on what Allen seems to be doing when he reads.

- Allen seems to focus on single letters or words, without thinking about what the whole message is about.

- When Allen comes to something that is hard for him, he has only one or two strategies to use, and those focus on the look and the sound of the word rather than the meaning.
- Allen does not seem to understand that he can use his background knowledge to try to figure out what he is reading.

So What Does This Mean?

As Allen's teacher shares what she knows about Allen, the other teachers suggest these questions to help her figure out what it all means for his literacy and what she can do for him.

- Can Allen play board games or computer games, where he would need to pay attention to the "big picture?"
- Can Allen tell stories about personal experiences?
- How does Allen participate in shared reading or writing activities?
- What is Allen's listening comprehension like?

Now What Shall We Do?

The Literacy Team talked about how to gather more information about Allen's literacy strategies. They also came up with suggestions about literacy engagements or instructional experiences that might help him focus on meaning. Next, they decided on literacy center activities that he might do independently. They also made suggestions for home support to provide Allen's parents with ways to help him focus on understanding what he reads.

Learning More About Allen

Retellings

Allen needs to understand that reading and writing make sense—that they tell a story bigger than single words and sentences. Anything you can do to get him to focus on meanings at the message level should help him with that. In the following instructional strategies, you can learn not only more about Allen and children like him, but you can help him understand more about the "big picture." In a retelling, after hearing or reading a message—narrative or expository—a student is asked to tell everything she remembers from the passage. A retelling should include main ideas and details, in the same sequence as the original message. It is different from a summary that includes only the essential information, leaving out elaboration and details.

Retellings can be written or oral. They may also be represented in art, drama, or dance. Retelling is an excellent assessment tool, but it is also an instructional strategy. Through successive retellings, students can build their proficiency in comprehension strategies. Retellings may be either free or structured. In a free retelling, the teacher simply asks the reader to tell everything she remembers from the message, and the student proceeds without prompting. A structured retelling can be based on an outline, a graphic organizer, or a series of pictures or other concrete representation designed to help trigger the retelling.

As an assessment procedure, the retelling can provide teachers and learners with a great deal of information. Obviously, a retelling demonstrates whether the reader understands and remembers the main ideas and the details of the passage. In addition, a retelling should also reflect the text structure of the original message. For example, a student's retelling of a story can suggest whether or not she understands that stories have a setting, characters, problems, and resolution. Or a retelling can indicate whether a learner understands that expository text can be an argument with a logical structure, with a particular sequence, and a particular relation between a conclusion and its supporting evidence. For these reasons, retellings provide a more useful assessment of comprehension than a list of comprehension questions.

Specific instructions for retellings, as well as an assessment rubric, are included in chapter 4.

Metalinguistic Interviews

Sometimes it helps to have a conversation with a child like Allen about how he thinks about reading and what strategies he uses. The interview questions in Figure 7.1 are adapted from the *Reading Interview* (Goodman, Watson, and Burke, 1987). Try to intertwine these questions into informal conversations as you read and write with children. Try to let them know that there are no wrong answers. You will also want to compare their answers to your observations of their reading and writing strategies. Sometimes they tend to tell you what they think you expect to hear!

Metalinguistic Awareness Inventory (Reading)

Adapted from the Reading Interview (Goodman, Watson, & Burke, 1987)

1. Who is a good reader you know?
2. What does _____ do that makes you say he/she is a good reader?
3. When you are reading and come to something you don't know, what do you do?
4. What else do you do?
5. Are you a good reader?
6. Tell me about what you do best as a reader.
7. What do you want to improve in your reading?
8. If you could spend time reading anything you want, what would you choose?

Metalinguistic Awareness Inventory (Writing)

Adapted from the Reading Interview (Goodman, Watson, & Burke, 1987)

1. Who is a good writer you know?
2. What does _____ do that makes you say he/she is a good writer?
3. When you are writing, do you ever have trouble thinking of what to say? If so, what do you do about it?
4. Are you a good writer?
5. Tell me about what you do best as a writer.
6. What do you want to improve in your writing?

Figure 7.1 Metalinguistic awareness inventory about reading and writing.

Literacy Engagements for Allen

The Literacy Team and Allen's teacher decided on several literacy engagements or instructional experiences that might help him pay attention to meaning when he reads. Next, they talk about related literacy center activities that he might do independently and suggestions for home support so that Allen can begin seeing that writing is fun and useful.

Rich, Detailed Book Introductions

For a child like Allen, the teacher needs to provide a rich, detailed introduction to the book before reading. According to Clay (1991), in order to draw him into the story, you may

- discuss the title and the author
- explain important concepts
- use the names of the characters in the discussion
- look at and talk about each picture
- elicit personal responses or experiences that relate
- use some of the new vocabulary in the discussion
- point out the words in the story
- draw attention to the structure of the text
- ask for predictions before reading

These introductory strategies help guide the reader to get an idea of the big picture before reading. Over time, observe the reader closely for independent use of these strategies. As the reader becomes more adept at paying attention to the author's message, the teacher can assume less and less of the responsibility.

Re-enactments

These are like retellings, except students act out what they remember from the story or other message. Students can actually do skits, with or without writing the dialogue first. Or they can use puppets or paper cut-outs to act out the events of the story (Wilhelm, 1997). They may choose to do timelines or maps to explain what happened in the story. This can be an impromptu check for understanding and can happen in a large group, with teacher direction. Or it can be a more involved small group activity, entailing rehearsals, costumes, and props. Either way, it is a great way to focus on the big meanings rather than on the words. For students like Allen this may be difficult, so it is important to give him lots of support as he learns how to re-create his understandings of what he reads.

Response Activities

We have seen teachers use many exciting ideas as they invite students to respond to literature. Here are samples of questions that can elicit those responses:

- What in this story made you laugh?
- What made you feel sad? Or angry?
- What would you say to this character if he were here right now?
- What did this story (or this event from the story) remind you of?
- Do you know anyone like these characters?
- What do you think will happen to these characters after the book ends?
- What do you think happened before the book began?

Some teachers have success with response journals, others have students write letters to one another, others encourage response in literature circles or book clubs, and others have students draw and paint their responses. The important point is to invite students to express how the literature made them feel or think, which is clearly different from finding the main idea or deciding what the author meant. With young children, teachers often lead this kind of discussion in a whole group setting. With lots of demonstrations and opportunities to participate, students will soon be able to respond more independently.

Sketch and Guess

Sketch and Guess is a response activity that would be especially helpful for Allen. After reading the same story or chapter from a textbook, students each choose a part to illustrate. You may ask them to choose their favorite part, the part that made them laugh, the part they could see in their "mind's eye," or the part that was most confusing. In pairs or small groups, students then share their pictures with one another and guess which part of the story is represented in each picture. Together, the group members can choose a line from the text to use as a caption for each picture. This activity requires that students think about the meanings as they read, to think about the meanings and represent them visually, and then return to the text and find particular sections.

Readers' Theater

Readers' Theater is a performance of a familiar or favorite story rewritten as a play. Students may write the script or scripts may be purchased. This strategy encourages not only writing but oral reading for a purpose. Oral reading fluency is enhanced with multiple rereadings. Since speaking, listening, reading, and often writing are included in a Readers' Theater activity, students are more likely to get the "big picture" of a story. Prepared scripts can be used but are not encouraged since students will benefit and take ownership from the writing of their own play. Nonfiction texts that include dialogue, speech bubbles, or how-to instructions can be used. Books from Joanna Cole's Magic School Bus series are excellent for Readers' Theater. Poetry which allows for two or more voices may be read and performed. Students may act out a story or even a nonfiction text such as a history text, that is read by a narrator. Although writing a play may seem a daunting task for a classroom teacher, start small; and as you and the students gain proficiency, your projects can become larger. So how do you get started?

- Students choose a favorite text or portion of a text to be written in play form.
- The teacher demonstrates how to turn the critical parts of the text into dialogue and how to determine which parts of the text need to be told by a narrator, or through dialogue or actions.
- Students and teacher work cooperatively to write and revise the text into a script.
- Props may be created but they are not necessary.
- Parts are divided among the students and should be read several times. Students should be encouraged to use actions to enhance the meaning of the script.
- Lines are not memorized but read from the script.
- Students perform the play for an audience.

Conceptual Maps

Children who do not get the "big picture" may not understand that messages have particular organizational structures that help readers get the point. Structures for narratives or stories are usually different from expository text, like that in science and social studies textbooks.

Allen might benefit from retelling stories in the form of story maps, story charts, cartoon strips, and so forth (see Figure 7.2). As he reads informational articles, he might see the big picture as he completes a conceptual map like those in Figure 7.3.

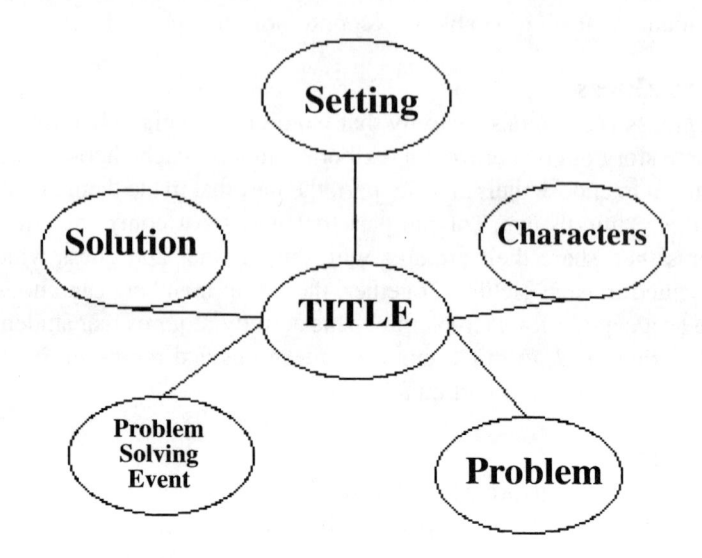

Setting	Characters	Goal	Problem	Solution

Figure 7.2 Story maps.

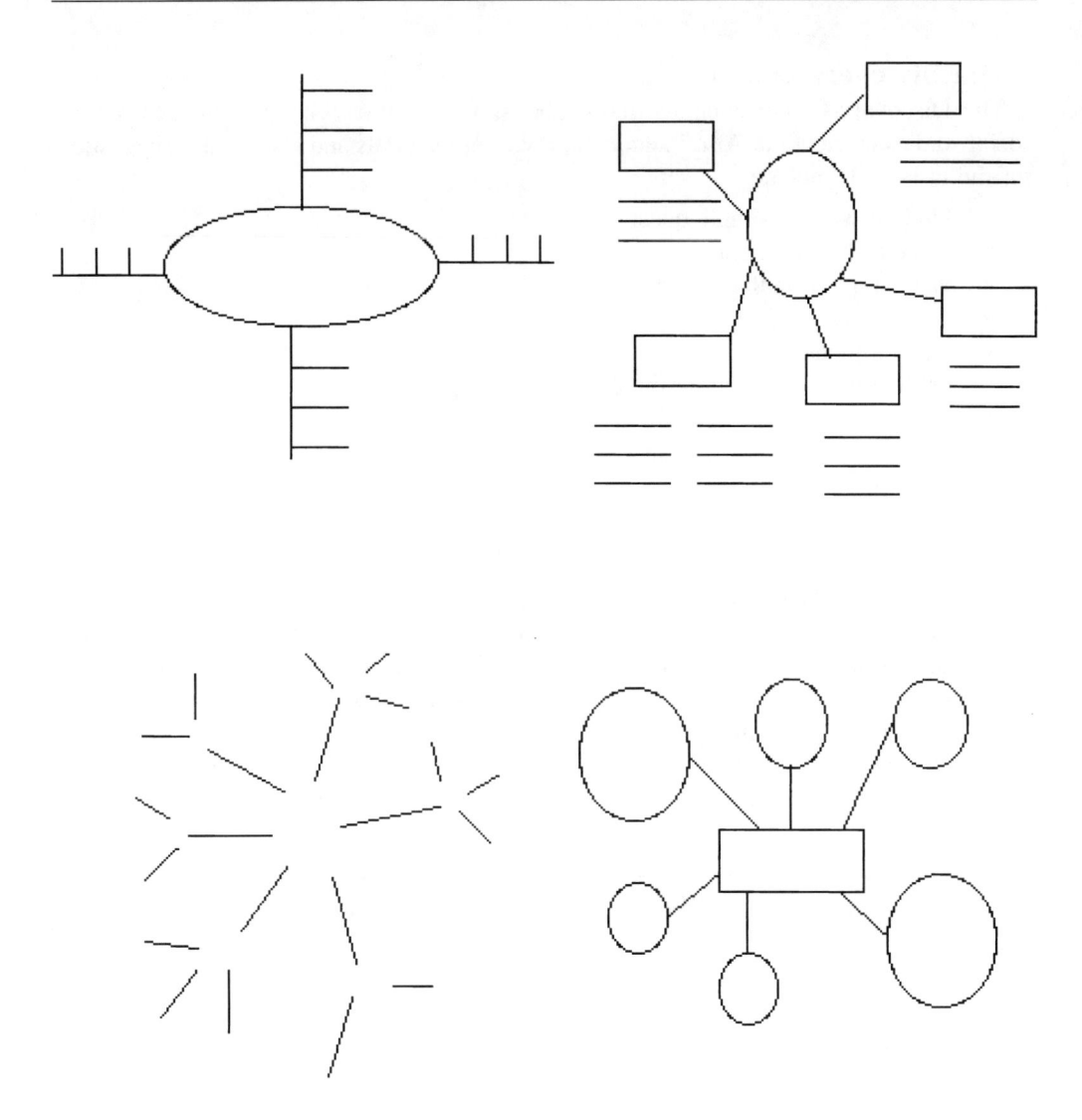

Figure 7.3   Conceptual maps.

Literacy Centers for Allen

The Writing Center

The Writing Center contains materials for writing such as various kinds of paper, small eight-page books already stapled together, markers and pencils, a stapler, staple remover, scissors, a file of pictures, familiar picture books for ideas, story map graphic organizers, lists of sample ideas, and folders for each student. At the writing center, children may create books with illustrations or cut out pictures, retell familiar stories, write about their own experiences, or write short reports on subjects they have read about. Students' writing is stored in folders and can be revisited for sharing, editing, and publishing.

The Discovery Center

The Discovery Center contains items, books, and pictures related to the science and social studies curriculum. Also included are writing materials and task cards. Suggestions for the task cards include

- Find answers to simple questions.
- Write a short description.
- Write a question that interests you.
- Write a list.
- Draw a picture.
- Draw a picture and write three facts.
- Create a chart.
- Talk to a partner about what you have learned.
- Write in your learning log.

Home Support for Allen

Encourage parents to read for 15–20 minutes a day with Allen. Also suggest that they talk about and retell movies and TV shows that they enjoy together. Simply talking about their plans for the day or reviewing what happened at the end of the day can provide some experience with retellings and focusing on sequences of events. You may want to copy and laminate the instructions in Figure 7.4 to send home in a book bag with library books for families to share together. Think about including a small spiral notebook with each book so that families can record their responses and read how other families have responded to that book.

How to Help Your Child With Reading

Before reading . . .
- Talk about what the book may be about—the title, author, and illustrator.
- Page by page, look through the book and talk about the pictures.
- If your child is reluctant to read to you, then read the book, pointing to each word with your finger. Direct your child's attention to the print and the pictures.
- Read the book to your child again, encouraging him or her to read with you.

During reading . . .
- Have your child point to each word as he or she reads.
- When a young reader makes a mistake that makes sense, don't worry about it.
- If the mistake doesn't make sense, wait to see if he or she will fix it.
- If not, you might listen until the child finishes the page or the section of the book and say, "Try this word again" or "Did that make sense?" or "Did what you read look right? Did that sound right?"
- Encourage your child to use the pictures to help with unknown words.
- Allow your child to skip an unknown word and read to the end of the sentence before making a guess.
- Encourage your child to be independent.
- Talk about what is happening in the story and ask questions.

After reading . . .
- Read the book again and again. Each time the reading should be easier and more fun.
- Talk about the characters, the setting the problem and how the problem is solved.
- Praise your child for his or her effort.
- Enjoy this time with your child and books.

Remember, you are your child's first teacher!

Figure 7.4 How to help your child with reading.

Resources for Further Inquiry

Clay, M. (1991). Introducing a new storybook to young readers. *The Reading Teacher, 45,* 264–273.

Gillet, J., & Temple, C. (1982). *Understanding reading problems.* Boston: Little, Brown and Co.

Irwin, J. (1991). *Teaching reading comprehension processes,* 2d ed. Needham Heights, MA: Allyn & Bacon.

Moore, D., Readence, J., & Rickelman, R. (1989). *Prereading activities for content area reading and learning.* Newark, DE: IRA.

Rhodes, L., & Dudley-Marling, C. (1988). *Readers and writers with a difference.* Portsmouth, NH. Heinemann.

Rhodes, L., & Shanklin, N. (1993). *Windows into literacy.* Portsmouth, NH: Heinemann.

Routman, R. (1991). *Invitations.* Portsmouth, NH: Heinemann.

Stauffer, R. (1975). *Directing the reading-thinking process.* New York: Harper & Row

Wilhelm, J. (1997). *You gotta be the book.* Portsmouth, NH: Heinemann.

Wolf, S. (1993). What's in a name? Labels and literacy in readers' theatre. *The Reading Teacher, 46* (7), 540–545.

Young, T., & Vardell, S. (1993). Weaving readers' theatre and nonfiction into the curriculum. *The Reading Teacher 46* (5), 396–406.

Chapter 8

Kids Who Don't Use Visual and Structural Cues to Make Meaning

Shaniqua loves to talk and tell stories to her teacher and her classmates. In fact, she often uses talk as a diversionary tactic to avoid reading and writing . . . or any other work that she is supposed to do. She is an active listener, enjoys being read to, and her speaking vocabulary is extensive. Yet her reading and writing skills are far below her classmates' and she knows it. Bright, playful, and articulate, she has figured out how to get the gist of what is read without being a strategic reader. Her retellings are often 70–80% correct, even with multiple miscues that should affect the meaning. In other words, she has not figured out how to use the graphophonemic cues in concert with meaning-making.

As she reads, her eyes dart all over the page searching for clues, rather than paying attention to the print. Although many of her miscues begin with the correct sound, she pays little attention to the rest of the word. She doesn't seem to make the connections between the classroom phonics instruction, the spelling patterns that she's been taught, and the printed page. She can memorize words in a pattern for a spelling test and then misspell the same word when she uses it in writing. Two- and three-syllable words are a mystery to which she has no key unless they have appeared in other stories that are very familiar to her.

Basals and trade books are used in Shaniqua's classroom for reading instruction. Although she has not mastered the first of the four leveled basals, the rest of the class is reading in the second and third books for the grade level. When she works in a group with the students who are reading on a higher level, she is confronted with text that she cannot read and, thus, either shuts down or becomes a behavior problem.

What Is Happening?

Shaniqua's teacher and her colleagues on the Literacy Team find it fairly easy to describe what Shaniqua seems to be doing as she reads and writes.

- Shaniqua is a risk taker who uses oral language to her advantage.
- Shaniqua is able to connect her background knowledge to print in order to make enough meaning to make up for her lack of reading ability.
- Shaniqua does not make logical predictions about words.
- Shaniqua is not able to talk about her reading or writing strategies.
- Shaniqua works hard to please her teacher and sees the literacy process not as a personal tool, but as a school task.

So What Does This Mean?

These are the questions Shaniqua's teacher and the other members of the Literacy Team ask as they try to figure out what to do for her.

- What does Shaniqua pay attention to during shared reading and writing?
- Does Shaniqua ever re-read books that she has previously listened to?
- Do books with predictable text support Shaniqua and allow her to make more reasonable predictions at the word level?
- Do the unconventional spellings in Shaniqua's writing show some sound/symbol correspondence?
- Does Shaniqua have a repertoire of known sight words?

Now What Shall We Do?

The Literacy Team talked about a how to gather more information about Shaniqua's reading and writing. They also came up with suggestions about literacy engagements and literacy center activities to help her use visual and structural cues. Finally, they generated a list of suggestions for home support for Shaniqua.

Learning More About Shaniqua

Modified Miscue Analysis

Miscue analysis and close observation while Shaniqua reads and writes will provide some more information regarding what she actually knows about how letters and sounds work to make meanings. Can she recognize words? Can she use initial sounds to make reasonable guesses? Does she ever self correct? Many teachers of young readers use "Running Records," as Clay (1993) explains in *An Observation Survey* of *Early Literacy Achievement*. Another procedure that accomplishes similar objectives is the Modified Miscue Analysis, based on the *Reading Miscue Inventory* (Goodman, Watson, & Burke, 1987).

Since we know that Shaniqua makes many miscues when she reads, the next step is to find out what types of miscues she makes. The modified miscue analysis is a procedure that makes it possible for the teacher to listen carefully to a student's oral reading, to see how the student is using the cueing systems to make meaning of the text. Taping the oral reading for later analysis can be extremely helpful. This gives both the teacher and the student a chance to focus on the words and phrases in the tape that don't match the text and to think about why the reader made those miscues. The miscues give us an idea about what cueing systems the reader is using to try to make sense of the text. They even give us an idea about whether or not the reader expects the language to make sense at all.

We have chosen to use a modified version of the *Reading Miscue Analysis* here. We explain it in more detail in *Framing Literacy: Teaching/Learning in K–8 Classrooms* (Mallow & Patterson, 1999). Whatever miscue analysis is used, it should be paired with a retelling so that the teacher can see the use of cueing systems in the context of how the student comprehends the whole text. A miscue analysis and a retelling provide a more complete picture of a reader's process and comprehension.

A miscue analysis gives a teacher a window into a reader's mind (Goodman, Watson, and Burke, 1987), an opportunity to see how the reader uses all the cueing systems as they move through a text. If the text says, "the house," and the readers says, "the horse," we know that the reader is looking at letters and sounds—the grapho-phonemic system. But we also know that the reader is paying attention to syntax because he substituted a noun for a noun. More importantly, if he doesn't go back and correct that miscue, we can be reasonably sure that he isn't trying to make sense, that he isn't paying attention to meaning. A miscue analysis is a systematic way to document how a reader is using the cueing systems. In this way, it can help a teacher make appropriate teaching decisions for individual students. Doing a miscue analysis can also help both the teacher and student understand more thoroughly how the reading process works.

Find a selection that is fairly difficult and new for the reader. It can be either narrative or expository text—a story or an informational, "explaining" piece. Introduce it to the reader with a sentence or two—to let the student know what it is about. Then say something like, "Please read this to me, and we'll record your voice on this tape. If you come to something hard, just do what you would do if I weren't here. I won't be able to help you this time. And when you are finished, we'll close the book, and you can tell me everything you remember about it."

Later, when you are by yourself, you can listen to the tape and mark a copy of the text with any miscues the reader made. After you mark the copy of the text, transfer the miscues and the correct word onto the analysis sheet. Remember that these markings are ultimately to help you make the best decisions you can about how to help this student. After you have recorded at least 25 miscues, you have enough to analyze. Here is how many teachers mark a copy of the text as the child reads or as they listen to an audio tape later:

Kind of Miscue	What the Text Says	What the Reader Says	How to Mark the Miscue
Substitution	The troll lived under the bridge.	The troll lived under the build.	The troll lived under the *build*/bridge.
Omission	The troll lived under the bridge.	The troll lived the bridge.	The troll lived ⟨under⟩ the bridge.
Insertion	The troll lived under the bridge	The old troll lived under the bridge.	The ^*old* troll lived under the bridge.
Self-Correction	The troll lived under the bridge.	The troll lived under the build . . . bridge.	The troll lived under the ©*build*/bridge.

Figure 8.1 Reading miscue inventory.

Once the miscues are marked, it is time to analyze them to see what the miscues can tell us about how the reader is using the cueing systems. For each miscue, answer these questions:
- Did the reader use graphic cues—or the letters in the word?
  (Are half or more of the letters the same?)

- Did the reader use the sound patterns in the word?
  (Are half or more of the sounds the same?)
- Did the reader use syntax cues?
  (Does the miscue sound "right" in the sentence? Or is there a grammatical fit?)
- Did the reader's miscues preserve the meaning of the sentence?
- Did the reader self-correct the miscues?

This analysis can give you dependable information about the reader's knowledge and use of the cueing systems.

Students do not "pass" or "master" a miscue analysis. There is not an ideal miscue result on any one passage because these results, even for one person, will vary depending on the nature of the text and the situation. The power of the miscue is that we can use it to identify patterns that can tell us about whether and how a reader is trying to make sense. Although a miscue analysis can give a detailed view of a reader's use of the cueing systems, it is an individual assessment and takes precious time. For that reason, many teachers use these procedures only with students who need extra help—the struggling students such as Shaniqua for whom the teachers need detailed assessment information. For other children, teachers may not do an actual written analysis, but teachers' knowledge of miscue analysis procedures

Summary Sheet: Retelling and Miscue Analysis

Student's Name:_____ Date:_____

Text:Title_____Length_____

Level (for this reader)   ____Hard   ____Instructional   ____Easy
Type of text: ____Narrative   ____Expository

Use of Cueing Systems: ____Strategic   ____Nonstrategic

    _____% of miscues are graphically similar to the text.
    _____% of miscues are phonemically similar to the text.
    _____% of miscues are syntactically similar to the text.
    _____% of miscues did not interfere with the meaning of that sentence.
    _____% of miscues were self-corrected.

Comprehension from Retelling:

	None	To a low degree	To a moderate degree	To a high degree
Repeats information directly stated in the text				
Includes the gist of the text				
Includes inferences based on information in the text				
Includes generalizations about the main problem or theme or thesis				
Attempts to connect reader's background knowledge with the text				
Attempts to apply generalizations based on the text to real world situations				
Includes affective or emotional responses to the text				
Organizes the retelling coherently				
Demonstrates as sense of audience				
Demonstrates control of the conventions of oral or written language				

Figure 8.2 Retelling and miscue analysis.

enable them to focus on students' oral reading "mistakes" differently. They can not only think about the strategies a student might be using, but they can also decide when to intervene and when to let the child continue making meaning independently.

Following is a sample miscue analysis, a transcript of the story with miscues marked, and a retelling rubic.

MODIFIED MISCUE ANALYSIS — SUMMARY SHEET

# Miscue / Text	Are half or more of the letters the same? Yes = ✓	Are half or more of the sounds the same? Yes = ✓	Does the miscue sound "right" in the sentence? (grammatical fit) Yes = ✓	Is the meaning of the sentence preserved? Yes = ✓	Does the reader self-correct? Yes = ✓
1					
2					
3					
4					
5					
6					
7					
8					
9					
10					
11					
12					
13					
14					
15					
16					
17					
18					
19					
20					
21					
22					
23					
24					
25					
Total # of ✓ marks					
Percentage # of ✓ marks divided by 25	%	%	%	%	

Figure 8.3 Modified Miscue Analysis—Summary Sheet.

TRANSCRIPT OF ORAL READING

We are using the complete text of *The Wing Shop* by Elvira Woodruff with permission from the author to demonstrate the marking and analysis of miscues and the retelling. Allen, a struggling reader in the third grade, read and retold the story. The child read the entire text in a school setting.

THE WING SHOP

Elvira Woodruff

     Man   finally
Matthew and his family had just moved from Main Street to Finley Street.
                        Marter
"I don't like it on Finley Street," thought Matthew. "It's too far from my old neighborhood. And nothing is the same." The house was different. "Too new looking," he thought. And the kids were
                                                                       slicky
different. "Too big looking," he thought. Even the porch steps weren't right. "Too skinny," he thought.
     Mardre   that
When Matthew asked his mother if they could move back, she just smiled and said, "This is our home now, you'll get used to it."

"Never," he thought.
  Mandrew
Matthew began to wonder just how he could get back to Main Street. He was too young to
                               a
drive a car. He was too little to take the bus alone, and his mother said he was not to walk past the drugstore.
          white Andrew   partagon
One day, while Matthew was playing outside, he began to follow a pigeon.
                                                                                          ©find
"If I had wings, I could fly back to Main Street," he thought. "But where can I get wings?" he wondered.
                         ~~partagon~~
    Mandrew   pigeon has fallen into par
Suddenly Matthew stopped. The pigeon had flown up to a pair of wooden wings hanging over
 floor
the door of a dusty old shop.
                                       Mandrew ©was
"Wings are just what I need," thought Matthew as he opened the door. Once inside he stopped
  started   never Sweeping   very
and stared. It was unlike any store he had ever seen. Swirling and flapping wings of every size,
   a   hang   a   shoelaces
shape, and color hung from the wooden shelves.

Kids Who Don't Use Visual and Structural Cues to Make Meaning

A very thin little girl with red fuzzy hair stood on a stool dusting a pair of chicken wings.

"Hello," said the girl. "My name is Lucy Featherman, may I help you?"

"Yes," replied Matthew. "I need a pair of wings."

"We've got plenty of those," Lucy said. "What kind do you need?"

"Well, I don't know," said Matthew. "Do you have a pair that can get me back to Main Street?"

The girl frowned and looked around the store. "I really don't know," she explained. "You see, I'm just watching the store for my grandfather. He went out to test some firefly wings last night and hasn't come back yet. Why don't you try on a pair?"

Matthew decided on a pair of lovely gray and white ones.

"Oh, you look wonderful," Lucy told him. "But don't you want to take off your socks and shoes?"

Just as Matthew bent down to untie his sneakers, a great gust of wind from an open window picked him up, and his wings began to flap! Before he knew it, he was flying out of the shop!

"Oh well, that's a good idea," said Lucy. Go for a test flight and see if you like them. Don't worry, they're guaranteed to bring you back."

But Matthew was worried! He had never flown before, and it felt very strange to be so far off the ground! He was flying high above the city's buildings. "This doesn't seem like the way back to Main Street," Matthew thought as he headed out to the harbor.

When he reached the ocean, the wings began to glide in close to the water. Matthew was having fun until the wings swooped down as if they were looking for fish.

Matthew's sneakers got soggy, his hair got wet, and he kept getting salt water up his nose! "I'll never get to Main Street this way," he thought. "I wish these wings would take me back to the store."

No sooner had he said that than the wings lifted him from the water and flew him to Finley Street. He sailed through the large window of Featherman's Wing Shop.

"Oh, I'm sorry," Lucy apologized, as she helped Matthew dry off. "I guess sea gull wings aren't really what you're looking for. I wish Grandpa were here to help."

As Lucy put the towel down, her hand rested on a shelf filed with leathery, black wings. "These might be just the thing," she said. *[lifty above "filed"; you need above "might be just the thing,"]*

"I'm feeling kind of seasick. Are you sure they're not sea gull wings?" Matthew asked as he tried them on.

"There isn't any tag, but I can look them up in Grandpa's inventory book, so we can tell just what kind they are," Lucy told him. *[inventually above "inventory"]*

But before she could open the large book, Matthew began to fly around the room. "I guess you'll have to give them a try," Lucy called as Matthew flew up and out the window.

This time the leathery black wings carried him far away from the city. Instead of flying to the ocean, Matthew was flying over fields and barns. He was in the country. He had never seen a real cow or pig before. "Moo, moo oinky, oink," he called down to the farm animals. But just as he was enjoying himself, the black wings scooped him through the window of an old barn. *[lelthy above "leathery"; stooped above "scooped"]*

Matthew found himself in the loft. It was hot and stuffy, and the wings had turned him upside down! "What kind of crazy wings are these?" Matthew wondered, as he swung from the rafters. "I wish they would take me back to the store." *[lot above "loft"]*

Just as he wished, the wings turned him right side up and flew him all the way to Finley Street. Matthew sailed through the big window and landed on the counter. *[Filly above "Finley"; slid above "sailed"]*

"I guess you didn't make it to Main Street," Lucy said in a rather small voice. BAT WINGS she wrote on a sticker and stuck it to the wings as Matthew took them off. *[ratter above "rather"]*

"I do wish Grandpa would mark these things," she said with a sigh. *[Do you above "I do"; sign above "sigh"]*

As Matthew sat down to rest, he noticed a small pair of gleaming airplane wings sitting on a display case. "If these were bigger, I bet they could get me back to Main Street," he said. *[©nockshed above "noticed"; "noticed" is boxed]*

Lucy helped pin them on. "Don't worry, the tag says expansible," she told him. No sooner had she pinned them on than they began to grow, and Matthew found himself zooming out the window! By the time he was above the street, the airplane wings had grown to full size. They were so big that they couldn't fit between the buildings. Matthew began to circle over the roofs. *[plan above "pin"; expound above "expansible"; snoop above "sooner"; pointed above "pinned"]*

"Stop," Matthew called to the wings. "There it is! There's Main Street!" But the airplane wings were much too big to land.

Matthew looked down at his old street and frowned. His house was where it always had been, but its big beautiful white porch was now painted a horrible pink. Even the steps were pink, except now instead of Matthew and his brother playing on them, three new children were there!

"Yuck," Matthew yelled. "What have you done to my house?"

"This is *our* house now. We live here, not you. Go away," they yelled back. [*your* written above *our*]

Before he knew it, Matthew was gliding over more houses and buildings. Suddenly he saw something below. "Hey, look down there," he called to the wings. [*it* written above *something*] "It's Finley Street! Hi, everybody," he shouted. He could see his whole family below him. His mother was hanging out clothes, his father was sitting on the porch reading the paper, and his little brother was playing on the steps.

Seeing them all together like that made Matthew smile. It almost made Finley Street look a little like his old home before all the pink. "Supper is ready," Matthew's mother called. [*Super* written above *Supper*] Matthew realized how hungry all this flying had made him. [*really* written above *realized*] He closed his eyes and wished himself back to the wing shop.

Suddenly the wings began to shrink, and before Matthew knew it, he was gliding through the big window of Featherman's Shop. [*shook* above *shrink*; *glidding* above *gliding*; *now* above *big*] He landed on the top shelf. Lucy had to help him down with a ladder.

"Did you get back to Main Street?" she asked.

"No, these wings are too big," Matthew said.

"Oh, I should have thought of that," said Lucy.

"Well, how about these? They're imported butterfly wings. You can get back to Main Street in style with these." [*important* above *imported*]

"Thanks," said Matthew. "But it's my suppertime now. And I don't think I can live on Main Street anymore. There are new kids living there, and my old house is not the same."

"Oh, I'm sorry," Lucy frowned. "But you know, I'd forgotten we were having a sale on bee wings today. Since you've been such a good customer, why don't you use these to get home, no charge." She smiled as she lifted a tiny velvet tray from the shelf. [*change* above *charge*; *velt* above *velvet*; *try* above *tray*]

      "Are you sure they'll take ~~me~~ [fluffy] home? Home to Finley Street?" Matthew looked wary [worry] as Lucy pinned the delicate [distance] little wings to the back of his sweatshirt.

      Suddenly ⊙there [these] was a great flurry of buzzing, as Matthew was lifted off the floor and out the shop's window! He hadn't gotten far when he zoomed down and hung dangling over the window box in front of the bakery. His face was in a geranium!

      "Good-bye," called Lucy from the window. "And remember, Grandfather is getting in new shipments [ships] all the time, so try and come again. Oh, and don't worry, you'll get home."

MODIFIED MISCUE ANALYSIS — SUMMARY SHEET

#	Miscue / Text	Are half or more of the letters the same? Yes = ✓	Are half or more of the sounds the same? Yes = ✓	Does the miscue sound "right" in the sentence? (grammatical fit) Yes = ✓	Is the meaning of the sentence preserved? Yes = ✓	Does the reader self-correct? Yes = ✓
1	slicky / skinny	✓	✓	✓		
2	that / this	✓		✓	✓	
3	won / our					
4	a / the			✓	✓	
5	white / while	✓	✓			
6	portagon / pigeon					
7	find / get			✓	✓	✓
8	has / had	✓	✓	✓	✓	
9	fallen / flown	✓		✓		
10	into / to	✓		✓		
11	par / pair	✓	✓			
12	floor / door	✓	✓	✓	✓	
13	was / as	✓	✓		✓	✓
14	started / stared	✓	✓	✓		
15	never / ever	✓	✓	✓		
16	sweeping / swirling	✓		✓	✓	
17	very / every	✓				
18	a / and					
19	hang / hung	✓	✓	✓	✓	
20	shoelaces / shelves	✓		✓		
21	ten / thin		✓			
22	should / stood	✓				✓
23	legs / wings			✓		✓
24	many / may	✓			✓	✓
25	shoes / sneakers			✓	✓	
	Total # of ✓ marks					
	Percentage # of ✓ marks divided by 25	68 %	40 %	60%	40 %	20%

SUMMARY SHEET: RETELLING AND MISCUE ANALYSIS

Student's Name: __Allen__ Date: __5/98__

Text Title: __The Wing Shop__ Length: Picture Book — 28 pages / Text on 21 pages

Level (for this reader): ✓ Hard ___ Instructional ___ Easy
Type of text: ✓ Narrative ___ Expository
Use of Cuing Systems: ___ Efficient ✓ Inefficient

__68__ % of miscues are graphically similar to the text.
__40__ % of miscues are phonemically similar to the text.
__60__ % of miscues are syntactically similar to the text.

__40__ % of miscues did not interfere with the meaning of that sentence.
__20__ % of miscues were self-corrected.

Comprehension:	Complete	Partial	None
• Retelling included main ideas.			✓
• Retelling included the details.			✓
• Retelling indicated an understanding of text structure.		✓	
• Retelling included evidence of inferencing and interpretation.			✓
• Retelling included evidence of connections with prior knowledge, like personal experiences and other reading selections.			✓
• Retelling included evidence of knowledge of terminology associated with literature, like "characters," "setting," "plot," "suspense," etc.			✓

Comments: Allen's miscues became somewhat less frequent as he read the story and he began to get the gist. His retelling was sparse, short on details and out of sequence. He did not want to add details when I reread his retelling to him. He called the name Matthew so many different things that I finally pronounced it for him. He used the pictures infrequently for meaning clues and seemed to view the reading process as mainly calling words. He never interjected ideas of his own. Allen is not a strategic reader and his inability to decode new words sometimes affects meaning.

Student Reflections

It may sound obvious, but we often forget that the learners have important insights into their strengths and weaknesses—insights that may come as a surprise to the teacher. If all else fails, ask the learner what she needs! These student reports and reflections can take many forms:

- Logs
- Reading records
- Response journals
- Interviews
- Think alouds
- Questionnaires
- Structured interviews
- Conversations and conferences
- Portfolio reflections

Asking learners to talk and write about their learning can help bring knowledge to a conscious level, so that they can self-evaluate and set goals. This leads them to take more ownership over their learning; it builds confidence and a sense of efficacy. When learners are able to talk about their knowledge and their strategies, we call this metalinguistic awareness. Metalinguistic awareness seems to lead to increasing control over literacy strategies, so that students can independently set purposes for reading and writing, choose appropriate strategies, and be successful in an increasingly wide range of reading and writing tasks.

Inexperienced readers and writers don't usually know how to do this metalinguistic reflection. Sometimes, teachers have to do some explicit instruction about what questions to ask as students have these "conversations with themselves." Here are some actions that teachers can take. Of course, these should be adapted to the interests and needs of particular students.

- Make reflective questions part of the daily routine in your classroom.
- Demonstrate how you reflect on your own reading and writing.
- Read widely and talk about the choices you notice that authors make.
    - What makes a story exciting?
    - What makes a nonfiction book easy to understand?
    - What makes a story realistic?
- Conversations exploring these questions can give kids criteria to use in self-evaluation and a vocabulary to use in their own reflections.
- Plan mini-lessons specifically on how to reflect, provide lots of opportunities to practice, and give students feedback on these early attempts.
- Provide opportunities for group reflection—in a class learning log or in evaluations of group projects—and for individual reflection.
- Connect reflection to self evaluation and goal-setting.

Some teachers make this a weekly routine. On Fridays, they ask students to look at their learning goals for the week, report what they achieved, and set new goals for next week. The teacher can set a number of group goals, and then individual learners can add their own. These goals may focus on accomplishing tasks or on learning specific concepts.

Literacy Engagements for Shaniqua

Choosing Appropriate Books

Shaniqua needs the structure and support of leveled texts for guided reading instruction and independent practice. Many schools today have built up libraries of multiple copies of small books that are leveled by difficulty. Teachers have worked together to level their existing books and have worked to raise money to buy multiple copies of books. Now, however, it is no longer necessary to make educated guesses about levels. Hundreds of books have been placed in 16 levels for kindergarten through fourth grade by Pinnell and Fountas (1996) in *Guided Reading*. These books are leveled according to the following factors:

- Length
- Size and layout of print
- Vocabulary and concepts
- Language structure
- Text structure and genre
- Predictability and pattern of language
- Illustration support

For help in leveling your existing books and stories in your basals, as well as future purchases of books, see chapters 9 and 10 and appendix M of *Guided Reading*.

Guided Reading

Guided reading is a teacher-guided instructional strategy in which small groups of children read a text for the first time. Although construction of knowledge of literacy is an individual process, it is often done in a social, supportive environment with more knowledgeable readers. Guided reading provides this support, especially with emergent readers as they make the transition into fluency. The purpose of guided reading is to enable children to read for meaning independently in increasingly challenging texts. Be sure to choose a leveled text that is developmentally correct for all the children in the group.

Select an appropriate text that is supportive and that offers only a few new things to learn. Prepare a brief introduction that will raise interest, relate the story to their interests and prior knowledge, and provide enough support to enable independent problem solving. Holding a copy of the book, introduce the book to the group by using some or all of the following elements:

- talk about the name of the story and the author;
- use aspects of the language of the story; talk about the names of characters; draw attention to the pictures building in story structure;
- draw out important concepts; and
- make personal connections and draw attention to various aspects of the print including words or phrases that may cause difficulty. (See also chapter 7.)

Vocabulary that is unfamiliar is not pretaught or drilled, but attention to the sound of the beginning letter may be focused as well as what would make sense syntactically or semantically. Engage the children in a conversation about the aspects of the introduction—encourage questions, observations, and predictions. Invite the group of children to read the whole book to themselves softly. During the reading, listen to, observe attempts, interact and help when necessary, and make notes of strategy use of individual students. Your help should always be unobtrusive and should lead the reader to make decisions based on both meaning and print.

After reading, discuss and ask for personal responses and connections to prior knowledge, guide reactions to predictions, point out successful problem-solving attempts, and use the time for short teaching interactions. After the first reading and discussion, a child may re-read the text with a buddy.

See Figure 8.3 for some things you can say to help readers build more strategies during assisted or guided reading:

Using graphic information
- Look at the picture to help you figure out the word.
- Do you remember that word in another story?
- Where have you seen that word before?
- Read the story using the punctuation.

Using grapho-phonemic information
- Do you think it looks like _____ (the miscue)?
- Look at how the word begins.
- Think about a word that has the same sound.

Continued . . .

Figure 8.3 Teacher prompts for use during guided reading.

- If that word was _____ (the miscue), what letter would you expect to see at the beginning? At the end?
- Does it look right? Does it sound right?
- Read that again to see if what you read looks right to you.
- You said_____ (the miscue). Point to the word. What can you see?

Using syntactical information
- Try that again.
- Does that sound right?
- You said _____ (the miscue). Can we say it that way?
- Would _____ fit there?
- Check to see if what you read sounds right to you.

Using semantic information
- Would that make sense?
- Put in a word that makes sense and go on. We'll come back to it later.
- Skip that word and read on. We'll come back to it later.
- Is that right? Check and see if that makes sense.
- Is that a word that you have heard before?

To help students talk about self-monitoring and self-correcting
- How did you know it was _____?
- Were you right?
- I like the way you worked on that by yourself. How did you do it?
- Can you find the tricky word that you had trouble with and tell why you had trouble? What do you think it is now?
- Why did you stop?
- What did you notice about that word?
- What part did not make sense?

Figure 8.3 (*Continued*) Teacher prompts for use during guided reading.

Remember that *guided reading is not a substitute for extended time devoted to independent reading and opportunities to respond to literature!* All beginning readers, especially those like Shaniqua, need lots of experience reading books and other materials they choose to read, either by themselves or with their friends. Guided reading, no matter how powerful, cannot substitute for that kind of independent reading.

Guided Writing

This activity is designed for work with an individual student who is experiencing difficulty in sound-symbol correspondence. Based directly on what has been observed in journal writing or what a child wants to write about a picture, the teacher prompts, guides, and reinforces what is known and, through modeling, supplies letter(s) as needed to complete a sentence. After the student states what he/she wants to write and the teacher has jotted it down, the teacher and student work on the sentence together, starting with the first word. The teacher uses guiding questions and prompts such as

- What can you hear in _____?
- What letter begins that word?
- Can you hear any other letters in _____?
- Can you write _____?
- Yes, it starts with a *b*.
- You are right, it does make an s sound, but it is written with a *c*.

For guided writing, the student writes with one color marker and the teacher uses a different color. As the sentence is written down, the known letters are written by the student and the unknown letters written by the teacher—always using guiding questions, statements, and modeling to lead the student to new understanding.

A guided writing sentence might look something like this: (The letters in italics were written by the teacher and would be in a different color on the original paper).

I l *i* ke t*o* go to the fa*r* m.

Guided writing is done on a separate piece of paper, dated, filed, and used for assessment purposes. Guided writing with one student can be done while other students are writing in journals, should not last over ten minutes, and the teacher's involvement should taper off as the student "takes off" on his own.

Cloze Activities

Another strategy that might be advantageous for Shaniqua is the cloze procedure. Using this procedure, the child is asked to read material from which words have been deleted. After the first complete sentence, usually every fifth word is omitted and replaced with a blank. The reader predicts or infers the missing words from context, relying on syntactic and semantic information (Does it make sense? Does it sound like language?). After reading on to the end of the sentence or even several sentences, the child either confirms the predictions or is required to re-read and suggest other words. Cloze is best used as a puzzle with multiple possible solutions.

Rewrite a passage from a book, deleting every fifth or seventh word, replacing it with a blank, leaving the first sentence intact.

- Ask the child to read the entire cloze activity before filling in missing words.
- Ask the child to read and predict what word would make sense in each blank.
- The word can be written in the blank or produced orally.
- Accept any word that would make sense in the blank.
- Children should share, compare, and defend choices, or reject and reread.
- Discuss the reason for the activity and the need for using background knowledge and context.

For additional support for the reader, the blanks can indicate length of the word (_____, _____), the number of letters in the word (_ _ _ _ _), or certain letters can be supplied (d _ _ , _ _ _ _ _ s). The words you choose to omit may vary with the students' needs: last word in the sentence, inflectional endings, function words, key concept-carrying words, only highly predictable words, grammatical classes such as verbs or prepositions. The cloze procedure may even be accomplished orally: as the teacher reads aloud, children follow along in a text and supply the next word at a signal from the teacher. This activity can be completed using a variety of texts such as poetry (rhyming words), content reading (key vocabulary), and stories (action or descriptive words).

Do not overuse this activity. It is best used as an illustration or demonstration of prediction. Most of the child's time should be spent reading real books rather than activities developed for reading instruction.

Literacy Center Activities for Shaniqua

Book Center
The book center contains several tubs of easy predictable books for independent practice. Students may read independently or with buddies. After they read, they may draw a picture about the story, write a summary, listen to a tape and read along, or tell another child about the book.

Word Study Center
The word study center should contain word tiles, words written on index cards, plastic or magnetic letters, an alphabet/word chart, handwriting books, markers, pencils, dry erase boards and markers, erasers, and any other supplies for a given activity. At the word study center students are expected to do any number of activities that will make them proficient in decoding, spelling, and writing words. For example, they may be expected to practice sight words with a partner, practice handwriting books, make words with plastic or magnetic letters, use word tiles or words written on index cards to create sentences, write a set of words in alphabetical order, practice writing words or manipulating plastic letters to create words that use the same pattern (for example, *-at, -ing*); sort sets of words written on index cards (for example, rhyming words, word families). Crossword puzzles, word games on the computer, and word searches can also be part of a word study center.

Home Support for Shaniqua
Parents need to be encouraged to read aloud to Shaniqua, with her sitting next to the reader who is pointing to the print. Predictable books with rhyme, rhythm, cumulative story structure, repeated refrains, and supportive pictures would provide enjoyment as well as scaffolding for Shaniqua as she joins in after repeated readings. Inviting her to join in for assisted readings repeatedly will force her to pay attention to the print. Rather than correcting any miscues, point out features of print, use your finger to cover parts of words, make a game of the reading and predicting. See the parent help chart in Chapter 7.

Resources for Further Inquiry

Clay, M. (1993). *An observation survey of early literacy achievement.* Portsmouth, NH: Heinemann.

Fountas, I., & Pinnell, G. (1996). *Guided reading: Good first teaching for all children.* Portsmouth, NH: Heinemann.

Goodman, Y., Watson, D., & Burke, C. (1987). *Reading miscue inventory: Alternative procedures.* Katonah, NY: Richard C. Owen Publishers.

Goodman, Y., Watson, D., & Burke, C. (1996). *Reading strategies: Focus on comprehension,* 2nd ed. Katonah, NY: Richard C. Owen Publishers.

Mallow, F., & Patterson, L. (1999). *Framing literacy: Teaching/learning in K–8 classrooms.* Norwood, MA: Christopher-Gordon.

Rhodes, L., & Shanklin, N. (1993). *Windows into literacy.* Portsmouth, NH: Heinemann.

Chapter 9

Kids Who Know About Letters and Sounds and Still Can't Read

Matt has always struggled to read. He actually began to read at the beginning of third grade when his special education teacher made time to read with him for 30 minutes daily as she learned about what he knew and built on that. Now, eight months later, Matt's oral reading is so slow and halting that, even in familiar books, he often loses the meaning by the end of the sentence. Although phonics instruction has been a regular part of his school routine since kindergarten, he remembers, connects, and uses little of what he's been taught when he reads. He uses little decoding knowledge, except some beginning consonant sounds, and he has a repertoire of about fifteen consistently remembered sight words. Matt is usually very quiet in class; and, when he does talk, his speech is halting and his vocabulary seems rather limited compared to other children his age.

Matt is highly distractable, even with his prescribed medication, and is a master at avoiding anything that requires him to read or write. He is mainstreamed into regular classes for science, social studies, music, and physical education; and those four teachers provide appropriate modifications for him. For example, the social studies teachers provides highlighted text and a reading buddy for him. His resource teacher teaches both math and reading/language arts. In Figure 9.1 are examples of sentences he composed, repeated, and wrote after reading parts of a self-selected, nonfiction book about dogs.

My	bakd	bok	was	gan	for	ferd	das	dat	we	kan	homd.
My	black	dog	was	gone	for	four	days	but	he	came	home.
a	bok	can	be	esel	to	tan.				
A	dog	can	be	easily	to	train.				
Fed	the	pae	for	tas	dat.					
Feed	the	puppy	four	times (a)	day.					

Figure 9.1 Matt's writing samples.

What is Happening?

Matt's teacher and the Literacy Team see a clear pattern in his reading and writing behaviors:

- Matt's oral language development is somewhat delayed.
- Matt is able to predict what the book will be about after looking at pictures, and connecting the pictures with his background knowledge.
- Matt shows little stamina or perseverance to complete a task.
- Matt uses some beginning letter sounds and picture cues to make meaning.
- Matt uses only a few spelling conventions.
- Matt often reverses b's and d's.
- Matt does not expect reading to make sense, and he does not seem to use literacy for personal purposes.
- Matt cannot talk about what he does or thinks about when reading/writing.

So What Does This Mean?

What Matt can't do seems to be evident to everyone. What we don't know is what he knows, likes, can do, or wants to do. At first glance, his education seems to be fragmented and possibly disjointed, because he works with as many as five teachers and two teaching assistants during a school day. The first thing that may need to happen is more communication among his teachers. The Literacy Team can provide a place for that to happen. Together, the Literacy Team members decide to explore these questions:

- How do we communicate to Matt that we expect him to be a successful learner?
- When does Matt show evidence of being an active learner, taking responsibility for his own learning?
- Does Matt rely more on visual or auditory cues when reading? when writing?
- Does Matt use drawing to support his writing?
- Is Matt willing to share his writing?
- Does Matt enjoy being read to?
- What do retellings reveal that Matt has understood from a selection that he has heard?
- What contributions does Matt make during a class discussion?
- What activities is Matt involved in after school?
- What interests does Matt have, inside or outside school?

Now What Shall We Do?

The Literacy Team talked about a how to gather information to answer these questions, and they brainstormed for suggestions about literacy engagements and literacy center activities to help Matt be more successful in all this classes. They also talked about how his family might help at home.

Learning More About Matt

Teacher Observations

The most important assessment tool in the classroom is the teacher. Through careful kidwatching (Goodman, 1978), teachers can focus on what their students can do and what they need to learn. This is especially important for students like Matt who have had academic struggles for several years. There are a number of ways these observations can be recorded:

- Anecdotal records
- Teacher's journal
- Checklists

When a knowledgeable teacher watches a learner closely over a long period of time, that teacher can come to know the student in a rich, multi-dimensional way. The key to using this information to make systematic decisions about instruction is to document the observations carefully. Focus first on strengths! Focus on what you actually see happening and try to avoid jumping to conclusions about the cause of that behavior. Watch for patterns over time and over a range of situations and different tasks. Supplement your observations with information from other sources, like student comments, parent comments, and work products. Try using tools to capture those moments in the rush of classroom life:

- Post-its
- Index cards
- Notebooks
- Status of the class chart
- Checklists

Make time to reflect on what the observations might mean. You may want to use a journal to record your reflections, or you may want to talk to colleagues. Many teachers are now using child study teams or critical friends groups to do that kind of systematic reflection to inform their instruction.

Conferencing

Besides your observations, conferences with students provide insights that otherwise might be overlooked or not observed. Donald Graves (1983) says that the purpose of the writing conference "is to help children teach you about what they know so that you can help them more effectively with their writing" (p. 59). That is just as true for reading conferences. Graves suggests that the unspoken message in the conference is that the student knows things that the teacher doesn't. The teacher's job in a conference, then, is to ask useful questions and to listen to the student's answers. Graves says that, for writing conferences, he comes to each student with three issues in mind:

- what the topic is about
- where the topic came from
- what the student will write next

In a similar fashion, we suggest that a teacher can come to a reading conference with these issues in mind:
- what the reading is about
- how the student responded to it
- the student's thoughts about why the author might have made particular decisions
- what was challenging or difficult for the reader
- what the student will read next

Sometimes conferences can be helpful at different points in the writing process—to choose topics, to revise for clarity or for elaboration, to proofread. Sometimes teachers prepare checklists or signature sheets to document how many conferences happened in the revision of a particular piece of writing. Those checklists, however, should not become ends in themselves. Spontaneous conferences are usually the most powerful because they address a particular need at just the right time.

We are including reading and writing conferences here as an assessment tool; but many teachers have found that conferencing is not only a great opportunity for individual assessment, but it is also a prime time for one-on-one instruction. There is not a single correct way to do conferencing. Teachers may schedule conferences with students in advance, attempting to sit down with each student individually at regular intervals. They may also make time for spontaneous conferences, sometimes called "squat conferences," that happen as the teacher is walking among the students to see who needs just-in-time assistance. Conferences may last from a few seconds to several minutes. Conferences can be with individuals or with a group of students who may need the same kind of help. Conferences are most successful when driven by student questions, but sometimes a conference offers a great opportunity for the teacher to teach a particular concept explicitly.

Most teachers have to learn to organize instructional routines so that the class can be busy individually or in small groups, allowing the teacher time for conferences. A businesslike atmosphere, explicit and consistent expectations for behavior, and engaging work for the rest of the class all contribute to helping the teacher manage conferencing as a regular part of the schedule. Conference records, kept in student folders or in a loose leaf notebook are also important tools.

Diagnostic Spelling Test

The following two diagnostic spelling tests can be used to document what young readers and writers know about sound/symbol correspondence, or how letters and sounds are used in decontextualized written language. Students can then be "taught" these elements within the context of reading and writing authentic messages and playing rhyming games. Here are suggestions for administering the spelling tests:
- Explain to students that you don't expect each word to be spelled correctly. You want to know how they think the words should be spelled.
- Read the word, then the sentence, then the word again.

Each of the diagnostic spelling tests can be given individually or to a whole class. The results of the test(s) can be used to plan spelling mini-lessons, when the need presents itself during the editing process of writing, and in decoding new words in reading. Additional words using the same phonics patterns, phonograms, or endings can be found in *The New Reading Teacher's Book of Lists* (Fry, Fountoukidis, & Polk,1985). Several times a year, you can examine the writing of the children and chart the spelling development of frequently used words as they move toward conventionality.

Diagnostic Spelling Test
List 1

Word	Sentence	Phonics element tested
1. not	He is not here.	Short *o*
2. bug	There is a bug on the door.	Short *u*
3. get	I need to get bread at the store.	Short *e*
4. him	Do you like him?	Short *i*
5. man	My daddy is a tall man.	Short *a*
6. boat	We took our boat to the lake.	Long *o*
7. train	The baby played with a toy train.	Long *a*
8. time	It is time to go home.	Long *i*-consonant-final *e*
9. cake	I like to eat birthday cake.	Vowel-consonant-final *e*
10. found	We found the lost ball.	*ou* diphthong
11. down	Be careful going down the steps.	*Ow* spelling of *ou* diphthong
12. soon	Soon it will be lunch time.	Long *oo*
13. good	This is good ice cream.	Short *oo*
14. very	It is very hot outside.	Final *y* as short *i* sound
15. my	This is my dog.	*Y* as long *i* sound
16. keep	We keep the colors in a box.	*K* spelling of *k* sound
17. come	Come to my house after school.	*C* spelling of *k* sound
18. what	What time is it?	*wh* digraph
19. those	Those are my shoes.	*th* digraph
20. show	Show me your picture.	*sh* digraph, *ow* spelling of long *o*
21. much	How much does it cost?	Final *-ch* digraph
22. sing	I like to sing.	Final *-ng* digraph
23. will	Will you ride with me?	Doubled final consonant
24. doll	I have a new doll.	Doubled final consonant
25. sister	My sister is older than I am.	*-er*
26. her	We gave her a present.	*-er*
27. toy	I gave him a toy for his birthday.	*-oy* spelling of *oi* diphthong
28. say	Please say your name clearly.	*-ay* spelling of long *a*
29. little	The little cat sleeps with me.	*-le* ending
30. one	My baby brother is one year old.	Phonetically irregular
31. would	Would you sit by me?	Phonetically irregular
32. pretty	That is a pretty picture.	Phonetically irregular

Figure 9.2 Diagnostic spelling test (List 1).

Diagnostic Spelling Test
List 2

Word	Sentence	Phonics element tested
1. farm	He grows cotton on the farm.	Medial *-ar*
2. mother	My mother is a doctor.	Voiced *-th* digraph, *er*
3. shoot	I want to shoot the BB gun.	digraph
4. straw	Let's drink the juice with a straw.	str blend, *-aw*

Continued . . .

Figure 9.3 Diagnostic spelling test (List 2).

5.	quick	She was quick to answer the question.	*Ou* spelling of *kw, -ck* ending
6.	third	She is in third grade.	Unvoiced *-th* digraph, *ir*
7.	bread	I like wheat bread.	*br* blend, *-ea* spelling of short *e*
8.	class	Our class is having a party.	*cl* blend, doubled consonant
9.	jump	Jump over the log.	*J* consonant sound
10.	jumps	The horse jumps the hurdle.	Addition of *-s*
11.	jumped	We jumped rope yesterday.	Addition of *-ed*
12.	jumping	Jumping is fun.	Addition of *-ing*
13.	skip	Please skip the next problem.	*Sk* blend
14.	skipping	She enjoys skipping.	Double final consonant, add *-ing*
15.	write	Write your name on the paper.	*Wr* spelling of *r* sound
16.	writing	She is writing in her journal.	Drop final e before *-ing*
17.	study	You must study for the test.	*St* blend
18.	studies	He studies every night.	Change final *-y* to *-i,* add *es*
19.	small	This is a small seed.	*Sm-* blend, broad *o* spelling of *a*
20.	smaller	This one is even smaller.	*-er*
21.	smallest	This one is the smallest seed we have.	*-est*
22.	afternoon	I want to go this afternoon.	Compound word
23.	grandmother	My grandmother likes to read.	Compound word
24.	can't	I can't wait to play at recess.	Contraction
25.	doesn't	He doesn't like to be quiet.	Contraction
26.	night	We go walking at night.	Silent *-gh*
27.	brought	Who brought the cake?	*Br* blend, silent *-gh*
28.	bugle	He played the bugle in the army.	*-le*
29.	again	Let's play the game again.	Phonetically irregular
30.	laugh	I love to hear her laugh.	Phonetically irregular
31.	because	We cannot go because of the rain.	Phonetically irregular
32.	through	They crawled through the pipe.	Phonetically irregular

Figure 9.3 (*Continued*) Diagnostic spelling test (List 2).

Literacy Engagements for Matt

Authenticity, Ownership, and Authorship

The authors of *Literacy Instruction for Today* (Au, Mason, and Scheu, 1995) state that ownership must the overarching goal for all learning and learners. Check your classroom and Matt's overall day at school for evidence of the following elements:

- Authenticity
- Making choices
- Setting own purposes
- Sharing
- Recognizing interests of others
- Connecting reading and writing
- Assessing one's own learning

Besides these elements of ownership, we would add the need for:

- Goal setting
- Acceptance of and acting on feedback
- Responsibility

All children, and especially children like Matt, need to have a goal in mind . . . to read a book, to finish a project, to start memorizing a poem (see chapters 3 and 4). Finally, Matt needs to accept the responsibility of acting on the feedback that he receives in the classroom, incorporating the teaching and suggestions into his reading and writing.

Conversations About Literacy and Language

Matt's problems with attention, his lack of literacy growth, and his subsequent behavior problems have led to his assignment to resource class. Not only is he isolated from his classmates when he goes to resource class, he is even isolated within the resource class, because his reading and writing skills and strategies are so far below that of the other students. Because of this, the social aspect of his literacy learning has been neglected. He could benefit from conversations about books, about read alouds, about his own and others' writing. He needs to be heard and to hear others. He needs to hear good books read aloud, chapter books that demand that his attention be stretched and picture books with beautiful language. His oral language needs to be developed with poems recited in choral reading and his experiences and writing need to be shared in class. He needs to write in many modes: lists, informative pieces about things he is interested in, personal narratives, directions, reports, poems, jokes, and letters. He also could be held responsible for leaving notes and messages for the other students and to the teacher. Pen pals in other classes or that you get off the Internet could stimulate a real desire to write for a real audience. Set up a mailbox in the classroom! He could spend time in the dialogue journal center and benefit in many ways with an ongoing written conversation with you, his teacher.

Since Matt has just begun to pay close attention to print, explicit teaching, using manipulatives (such as magnetic letters, word cards, letter cards, dry erase boards and markers) with specific word recognition activities seems to be called for. See word study activities in chapter 5.

Interactive Writing

Interactive Writing is a teacher guided group activity designed to teach children about the writing process and how written language works (Pinnell & Fountas, 1998). The teacher and children compose and "share the pen" as they think and write together. Children are invited to write word parts or whole words, with the teacher filling in the rest. Interactive writing can be used to demonstrate and involve children in any or all of the purposes of writing such as lists, descriptions, retellings, labels, letters, directions, recipes, graphs, charts, observations, and stories. Here is the routine, framed as a Daily News Story:

- Gather the children on the rug in front of a chart tablet on an easel.
- One child tells some news and all repeat it several times.
- Negotiation between teacher and students can occur about how to write the news.
- Invite a child to the chart to begin the writing with a colored marker.
- All say the first word slowly, sounding out and blending the sounds slowly.
- Have an alphabet chart nearby for handy reference.
- The teacher and child share the pen in writing the message.
- The teacher chooses different children to write each subsequent part of the message by asking "Who can write . . .?"
- If a child writes a letter or letters that need to be corrected, allow time for self-correction, ask a question that can lead to a correction such as, "Does that look right?" or quickly cover the errors with correction tape, and write the correct letter(s).
- Reread each word as writing is done, constantly reminding and demonstrating how a writer must work one word at a time while keeping the whole message in mind.

- As writing continues, have students refer to the word wall, name chart, and environmental print in the room.
- Have one child use a tongue depressor to clearly create space between each word.
- Choose teaching points and model strategies.
- Bring attention to how words and word parts look.
- Be sure to make connections between known and unknown words.
- Constantly point and re-read, check for number of words and correctness when finished.

This is a great opportunity to do some explicit teaching of points that the children need to have demonstrated for them. Here are some possible teaching points:

- Where to begin writing
- Directionality of writing
- Beginning sounds
- Print concepts such as word, upper and lower case letters, spacing
- Re-reading to figure out what to write next
- Punctuation marks
- Sound sequencing in words
- Parts of words
- Counting and clapping syllables
- Return sweep
- Add new words to the word wall

Assisted Reading and Repeated Readings

Like Tiffany in chapter 3, Matt could benefit from assisted reading, that gives the student an opportunity to read along with the teacher or another fluent reader (preferably with training and practice in this procedure). Using fluent oral reading as a vehicle, the ultimate goal of assisted reading is fluent silent reading. See chapter 3 for specific procedures.

Repeated reading is a technique for increasing reading fluency. It is used in an assisted reading situation with either an adult reading a selection aloud multiple times with the child or having the child read along with a tape of the text. The use of repetition is based on the observations of children who ask for books to be read repeatedly until the text is memorized. Repeated reading helps increase two of the elements of fluency-rate and accuracy. With children such as Matt, who labor over accurate word calling, using the appropriate stress, pitch of voice, and juncture between words is difficult. This can best be accomplished using poems, songs, or highly predictable texts that have rhyme, cumulative story structure, and/or a refrain that is repeated.

Literacy Centers for Matt

Dialogue Journal Center

This center is set up as a place where students may write to the teacher and expect a written reply. Dialogue journal communication is sometimes referred to as written conversation, where the focus is on meaningful, purposeful written dialogue about topics of interest, not on conventions or instruction of literacy. Each child's journal should be located at the center with a convenient tray for putting the journal when the student is through writing and wants a response from the teacher. For children who are reticent, the teacher may need to begin the dialogue. The students can be encouraged to include drawings with their writing. With an authentic audience and an authentic purpose for writing, many children such as Matt can be empowered to take risks in literacy.

Listening Center

The listening center was suggested for Tiffany in chapter 1, but it would also be powerful for Matt. Matt needs lots and lots of experiences hearing book language as he follows along with the text. Matt can read along orally while listening to a tape. Multiple rereadings lead to fluency and increased comprehension. Since this is a fairly noisy activity, this center might be situated behind a short bookcase or a rolling bulletin board. Re-readings will be especially helpful for Matt. Also, chapters from the science and social studies texts can be taped and placed in the Listening Center so that students like Matt who have a hard time reading on-level text can have this additional way to access the information in textbooks.

Home Support for Matt

Matt needs authentic uses for family literacy. He could keep a chart on pet care, chores around the house, car maintenance, and homework. His parents need to read with him and provide paper and pencils for writing. He could be put in charge of keeping a running list of groceries that are needed. All environmental print needs to be pointed out to him when the family is in the car. He should be held responsible for his homework and for doing his chores without being reminded.

Resources for Further Inquiry

Au, K., Mason, J., & Scheu, J. (1995). *Literacy instruction for today.* New York: HarperCollins College Publishers.

Calkins, L. (1990). *Living between the lines.* Portsmouth, NH: Heinemann.

Calkins, L. (1994). *The art of teaching writing.* Portsmouth, NH: Heinemann.

Carroll, J., & Wilson, E. (1993). *Acts of teaching: How to teach writing.* Englewood, CO: Teacher Ideas Press.

Fry, E., Fountoukidis, D., & Polk, J. (1985). *The new reading teacher's book of lists.* Englewood Cliffs, NJ: Prentice Hall.

Glazer, S. (1998). *Phonics, spelling, and word study: A sensible approach.* Norwood, MA: Christopher-Gordon.

Graves, D. (1983). *Writing: Teachers and children at work.* Portsmouth, NH: Heinemann.

Graves, D. (1994). *A fresh look at writing.* Portsmouth, NH: Heinemann.

Pinnell, G., & Fountas, I. (1998). *Word matters.* Portsmouth, NH: Heinemann.

Chapter 10

Kids Who Have Little Experience with "School" English

Rosa was nine years old and spoke only Spanish when she entered public school in the United States. She was placed in a third grade dual language (Spanish/English) classroom. She had moved from a rural area in Central America, where she had spent about two years with her family in hiding, waiting to receive political asylum in the United States. Rosa had never been to school, but her parents had worked with her to help her begin learning to read in Spanish. Both parents and her two older brothers are also learning English.

Her teacher immediately realized that Rosa had had little exposure to English literacy other than environmental print. She does, however, know how to write her name and can recognize the logos of American products sold in her country. Rosa knows the purpose of print and the names of some of the letters in Spanish. She can follow along with choral readings in Spanish. Her oral Spanish is well-developed, and she appears to be overcoming her initial shyness and is beginning to talk to classmates. Rosa is a careful listener, and her parents report that she is trying out English phrases at home. She listens attentively when the teacher reads aloud in English; and, during free reading time, she often chooses the read aloud book, especially if it is a picture book.

What Is Happening?

Rosa's teacher explains what she is seeing to the other members of the Literacy Team:

- Rosa has a strong first oral language base on which she can build her second language learning—both oral and written.
- Rosa is beginning to learn to read in Spanish.
- Although Rosa experienced some traumatic times before her family moved here, she seems relaxed and happy in her new home.
- Rosa takes the risks to try to speak English phrases at home.
- Rosa listens attentively to English and wants to look at story books in English, especially those the teacher has read aloud.
- Rosa is beginning to feel comfortable with her school friends.

So What Does This Mean?

The Literacy Team helps Rosa's teacher think about what all this means for the special support Rosa might need at this new school.

- In this bilingual classroom, Rosa can continue to learn to read and write Spanish as she learns to read and write English.
- In a supportive environment, Rosa can learn to use what she knows about language to build knowledge and strategies in both languages.
- Because Rosa is in a dual-language classroom, she can continue to learn content, even though her written and oral English proficiency is not as strong as her classmates'.
- Although Rosa can participate as a listener in many of the class activities, she may need some one-on-one instruction on specific strategies.
- Because Rosa's entire family is learning English, the time she spends hearing and responding in English at school is very important.

Now What Shall We Do?

Although Rosa needs to be included with her classmates in their reading and writing experiences, the Literacy Team helps Rosa's teacher think about specific activities that she might emphasize for Rosa, as well as the Literacy Centers and the home support which might be most helpful for Rosa.

Learning More about Rosa

Close kidwatching is the best way to assess Rosa's strengths and needs. All the assessment strategies suggested in previous chapters might be helpful. In addition, Figure 10.1 provides a set of questions that have been developed and tested with students learning to read English as their second language.

Strategy Interview

Renee Rubin has taught bilingual and biliterate students in south Texas for several years, and she is now focusing her research on how biliterate learners use strategies in their first language as they develop strategic reading behaviors and attitudes in English. Most of Renee's students speak and read Spanish as their first language. She has adapted other interviews (Jimenez, Garcia, & Pearson, 1996; Padron & Waxman, 1988) for these particular students and has developed the interview found in Figure 10.1:

Reading Strategy Interview for Students Who Read Spanish and are Learning to Read English

Gather both Spanish and English reading materials to appeal to a range of reading levels and interests, and arrange them on the table in front of the student. Then ask these questions and tape record the responses if possible:

1. Please look at all these materials and divide them into one pile that you would like to read and one pile that you would not like to read. When you have finished, explain your decisions.
2. Do you read in your spare time? Why or why not?
3. What do you like to read?
4. Do you know someone who is a good reader? Tell me why you name that person. What do they do to make you think they are good readers? Do they read in Spanish or English or both?
5. What do good readers do when they read?
6. When you are reading and you come to something you don't know, what do you do? (Follow up by asking what else they do.)
7. Are you ever able to say the words but not know what it means?
8. Are you a good reader in Spanish? How did you become a good Spanish reader?
9. Are you a good reader in English? How did you become a good English reader?
10. What do you notice that is the same about reading in Spanish and in English?
11. What do you notice that is different?
12. How does being able to read in Spanish help you when you read English?
13. How does being able to read in English help you when you read Spanish?

Figure 10.1 Reading Strategy Interview.

An interview like this is best used in bilingual classrooms where the teacher can translate the questions to Spanish as needed. Rosa, for example, may not know enough English to be able to answer these questions completely. In ESL settings, it would be difficult to use this interview until the student had reached a certain level of fluency in oral English. This interview does, however, point out the connections between the languages that both teachers and students look for.

Literacy Engagements for Rosa

Rich Oral Language and Literacy Opportunities

Language and literacy learning proceeds in much the same way in Spanish and in English. In dual classrooms, children are exposed to opportunities for learning two languages, and also to opportunities to use two languages as they learn about the world inside and outside their classrooms.

The goal is to build reading and writing strengths in the child's first language so that they can use those strengths as they read and write in the second language. Recent research strongly suggests that there is no reason to wait until children's oral performance in the first language is fluent before beginning to read and write in the second language. Here are some principles from the research on second language learning:

- *Language must be meaningful, interesting and connected to the child's background, interests, and needs.* Knowledge of words and concepts is grounded in action and experience, and children learn language by using it in real communication situations.
- *Children can understand oral language before they talk or write it.* Oral and written language involves two-way communication; people learning a second language typically listen a long time before they begin trying to produce the language.
- *Listening, speaking, reading, and writing are interrelated in complex ways.* Oral language does not need to be fully developed before writing. Oral reading fluency may not be a good indicator of reading comprehension.
- *Recognize that the home culture is essential to the learner's identity.* Honor the home language and culture as you bridge to the new language and culture.
- *Use assessment strategies that build on strengths of children.* Avoid depending only on standardized measures that foreground students' deficits.
- *Provide frequent hands-on experiences with lots of accompanying talk.* Connect the known to unknown. Provide real-life learning experiences with field trips and explicitly teach vocabulary based on those concrete experiences.
- *Regard errors as part of learning.* Support learners as they make attempts to learn the new language. Celebrate approximations, providing feedback that informs the learners about what to say or write the next time.
- *Allow time for thought, translation, and response.* Give wait time for answering questions.
- *Talk about strategies,* about the similarities and the differences in the languages. Encourage attention to the differences between their first and second languages. That kind of talk gives students a higher level of metalinguistic awareness and potentially greater control over their language and literacy strategies.
- *Provide group work,* time to talk, and to share writing and responses to literature. Provide real audiences and tasks that require language use.
- *Recognize the teacher's powerful role* as a language user. Model appropriate usage and syntax. Demonstrate a range of literacy uses. Think aloud about your strategies.
- *Build a climate to support risk-taking.*

Choral Reading

Choral reading of poems, songs, or texts written specifically for choral reading provides an ideal context for repetition with small groups or whole group participation. The students read a selection with alternating arrangements in choral fashion. This is best done with the selection written in large print on chart paper or by providing a copy of the text for each reader. Repeated readings in choral fashion can be done in unison, in small groups reading alternating lines, or with individual students reading alternating lines. When pictures, actions, or props are added to the chart, comprehension is heightened.

The *Sounds of Language* (Martin, 1991) series published by DLM has many excellent selections for choral reading. Another resource, written for second-language learners but providing any learners practice with the rhythms of English, is *Jazz Chants* (Graham, 1979).

Drawing

As people learn a second language, it is often helpful to use both written language and illustrations to communicate. That may mean that teachers present lots of drawings to support content area instruction. It may mean the students are asked to (or allowed to) draw their answers to test questions or vocabulary quizzes. It may mean that murals, dioramas, charts, models, sketches, and so forth, may be the best way for students to show their comprehension of written text.

Video and Multi-media

Another way to help students use multiple images and symbols to communicate is through multimedia. Many computer programs now allow students to combine words and icons to tell stories and to explain what they know about topics in science and social studies. Using videos, with or without subtitles can also be a way to support students' meaning-making as they become more proficient with the written language.

Mind Mapping

Mind mapping is a way of representing concepts with a graphic organizer and drawings. In mind mapping, a reader uses words, lines, color, and drawings to organize, sequence, connect, and remember important elements and ideas. Using the combination of auditory,

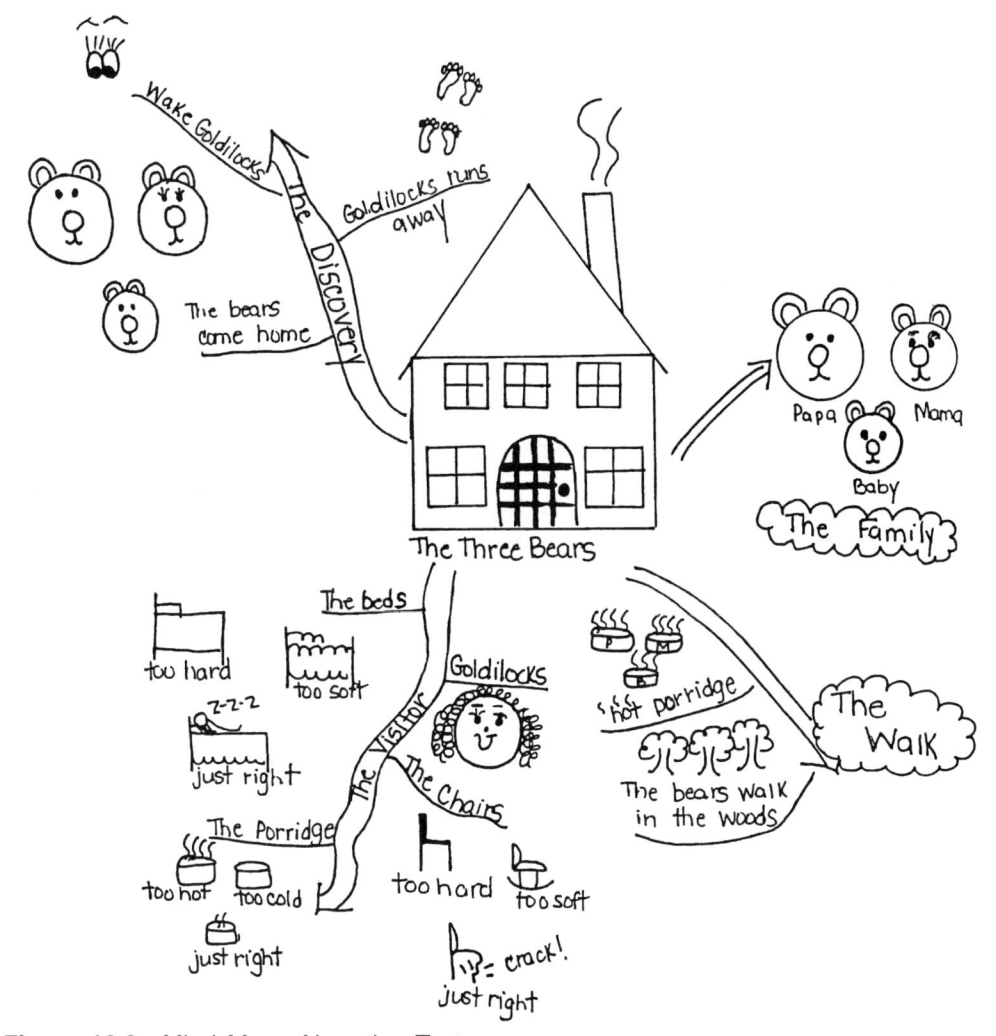

Figure 10.2 Mind Map—Narrative Text.

Figure 10.3 Mind Map—Expository Text.

kinesthetic, and visual modalities to create a mind map develops active thinking, verbalization, creativity, and memory. Mind maps are great tools for students like Rosa, as they learn a new language, learn concepts in both languages, and learn new words for familiar concepts (Buzan, 1983; Margulies, 1991; Williams, 1991).

The map is developed with the title or main idea circled in the middle, with branches representing key ideas radiating out from the circle. The branch, key words, and drawings for each branch can be represented with a different color. Each branch is labeled and words for important details are connected to the branch. Boxes can be put around words. Lines and arrows can connect elements of the mind map. Every written label and detail is accompanied by a drawing or cut-out picture to represent it. Mind maps can be demonstrated by the teacher, developed by the whole class, created in small groups, or by individual students. See the examples in Figures 10.2 and 10.3.

Literacy Centers for Rosa

Environmental Print Big Book Center

The Environmental Print Big Book Center contains a big book of logos of familiar products, store names, names of toys that are popular—all of which have been cut out, mounted on large construction paper and laminated for use in the center. The activities for this center are endless: use a pointer and read the print, match the logo with a card that has the typed name, match the store name with plastic toys representing items that can be purchased at the store, or match the product name in the big book with the actual product in the class store.

Art Center
The art center should contain various materials from which children can create a visual response to the reading. Ideas for responses on a posterboard can form a backdrop for the center. Students should know how to use all the materials and how to clean up and display their products when they are finished. Materials might include a stapler, scissors, crayons, white and colored paper, assorted boxes of different sizes, butcher paper, posterboard. Discussion and sharing of the product further enhances the response to the story. Using art can be a motivator to for a child who struggles with the printed word.

Home Support for Rosa
Rosa's family is clearly supportive and wants her to be successful at school. Perhaps the best way to think about families like Rosa's is to look at them as learning resources for you and your students. Luis Moll, Norma Gonzales and colleagues (1992) have done research on the "funds of knowledge" in families and communities in elementary schools in the Tucson area. The teachers and researchers do home visits to find out what the families know that can become resources to support the curriculum. When we did a similar project in the Houston area, teachers and family members became friends and it changed the way the teachers made decisions about all their children. You can read about that project in *Networks: An On-line Journal for Teacher Researchers* (Patterson & Baldwin, 1999) (http://www.oise.utoronto.ca/~ctd/networks/).

Resources for Further Inquiry

Au, K. (1989). *Literacy education in multicultural environments.* New York: McGraw-Hill.

Clayton, J. (1996). *Your land, my land: Children in the process of acculturation.* Portsmouth, NH: Heinemann.

Fu, D. (1995). *"My trouble is my English" Asian students and the American dream.* Portsmouth, NH: Heinemann.

Freeman, D., & Freeman, Y. (1994). *Between worlds: Access to second language acquisition.* Portsmouth, NH: Heinemann.

Genesee, F. (1994). *Educating second language children: The whole child, the whole curriculum, the whole community.* NY: Cambridge University Press.

Graham, C. (1979). *Jazz chants for children: Rhythms of American English for students of English as a second language.* New York: Oxford University Press.

Jimenez, R. T., Garcia, G. E., & Pearson, P. D. (1996). The reading strategies of bilingual Lantina/o students who are successful English readers: Opportunities and obstacles. *Reading Research Quarterly, 31,* 90–112.

Moll, L., Amanti, C., Neff, D., & Gonzalez, N. (1992). Funds of knowledge for teaching: Using a qualitative approach to connect homes and classrooms. *Theory Into Practice, 31,* 132–141.

Patterson, L., & Baldwin, S. (1999). Claiming our ignorance and making new friends. *Networks: An On-line Journal for Teacher Researchers, 2,* 2. (http://www.oise.utoronto.ca/~ctd/networks/).

Chapter 11

Solving Puzzles, Changing Lives

When children don't learn to read at five or six or seven, we shouldn't panic. Reading is a complex and individualistic process, and there is no one time table and no one path to literacy. When given the chance and appropriate support, children move toward fluency, confidence and independence in many different ways. It is hard for us to remember that, however, when teachers feel an intense public pressure to have all children reading "on grade level" (whatever that might mean). That political reality is inescapable, and it means that we must work together to puzzle out how we can best support all children in their unique journeys toward mature literacy.

Solving these puzzles together is often messy—with false starts, dead ends, and sudden, breath-taking discoveries. That is why we suggest that you and your colleagues build a Literacy Team on your campus. Just be aware that effective Literacy Teams do not just happen. They take thoughtful work on the part of administrators and teachers. Sharon Lewis (2000) studied the development of campus Literacy Teams, focusing particularly on one successful team on a campus in a suburb of Houston, Texas. She noticed that these teams went through a developmental process paralleling human growth through "infancy," "adolescence," and "adulthood." As you begin the literacy team process, you can't expect new teams to function the same way they will three years later. New teams may need more structure and more support from a lead teacher or consultant. As teams move into "adolescence," they are gaining in their expertise and independence so they may need different resources from the administration and different support from those in leadership positions. It took three years for the team Lewis studied to begin showing "adult" characteristics—with team members calling meetings and setting agendas on their own, sharing leadership among them, and using what they were learning about the individual students to make recommendations for campuswide curriculum and staff development projects.

Literacy Teams are worth the effort because everyone wins:

- Administrators have one more way to learn about what's going on to help children on the campus.
- Parents receive more detailed information about their child's literacy.
- Teachers have access to a deeply challenging and rewarding professional experience.
- Children benefit from the combined expertise and experience of all the Literacy Team participants.

Every child learns. Every child has a chance to become joyfully and independently literate. And that is certainly worth the effort.

References

Ashton-Warner, S. (1963). *Teacher.* New York: Simon & Schuster.

Au, K., Mason, J., & Scheu, J. (1995). *Literacy instruction for today.* New York: HarperCollins College Publishers.

Buzan, T. (1983). *Use both sides of your brain.* New York: E. P. Dutton, Inc.

Calkins, L. (1990). *Living between the lines.* Portsmouth, NH: Heinemann.

Carr, E., & Ogle, D. (1987). K-W-L plus: A strategy for comprehension and summarization. *Journal of Reading, 30* (7), 626–631.

Clay, M. (1991). Introducing a new storybook to young readers. *The Reading Teacher, 45,* 264–273.

Clay, M. (1993). *An observation survey of early literacy achievement.* Portsmouth, NH: Heinemann.

Clay, M. (1998). *By different paths to common outcomes.* York, ME: Stenhouse Publishers.

Fry, E., Fountoukidis, D., & Polk, J. (1985). *The new reading teacher's book of lists.* Englewood Cliffs, NJ: Prentice Hall.

Goodman, K. (1996). *On reading.* Portsmouth, NH: Heinemann.

Goodman, Y. (1978). Kidwatching: An alternative to testing. *National Elementary Principal, 57,* 41–45.

Goodman, Y. (1980). The roots of literacy. In M.P. Douglas (Ed.), *Claremont reading conference 44th yearbook.* Claremont, CA: Claremont Graduate School.

Goodman, Y. (1986). Children coming to know literacy. In W. Teale & E. Sulzby (Eds.), *Emergent literacy: Writing and reading* (pp. 1–14). Norwood, NJ: Ablex Publishing Corporation.

Goodman, Y., Altwerger, B., & Marek, A. (1989). *Print awareness in pre-school children.* Program in Language and Literacy, Arizona Center for Research & Development. Tucson: University of Arizona.

Goodman, Y., Watson, D., & Burke, C. (1987). *Reading miscue inventory: Alternative procedures.* Katonah, NY: Richard C. Owen Publishers.

Graham, C. (1979). *Jazz chants for children: Rhythms of American English for students of English as a second language.* New York: Oxford University Press.

Graves, D. (1983). *Writing: Teachers and children at work.* Portsmouth, NH: Heinemann.

Griffith, P., & Olson, M. (1992). Phonemic awareness helps beginning readers break the code. *The Reading Teacher, 45* (7), 516–523.

Hall, N. (1987). *The emergence of literacy.* Portsmouth, NH: Heinemann.

Halliday, M. K. (1973). *Explorations in the function of language.* London: Edward Arnold.

Harste, J, Woodward, V., & Burke, C. (1984). *Language stories and literacy lessons.* Portsmouth, NH: Heinemann.

Holdaway, D. (1979). *The foundations of literacy.* Sydney, Australia: Ashton Scholastic.

Hoskisson, K., & Krohm, B. (1974). Reading by immersion: Assisted reading. *Elementary English, 51,* 832–936.

Jimenez, R. T., Garcia, G. E., & Pearson, P. D. (1996). The reading strategies of bilingual Lantina/o students who are successful English readers: Opportunities and obstacles. *Reading Research Quarterly, 31,* 90–112.

Lewis, S. (2000). *Evolution of a Reading Recovery© literacy team: A systemic, schoolwide approach to early intervention.* An unpublished doctoral dissertation, University of Houston.

Mallow, F. (1993). *The writing development of kindergarten children in ESL and the changes in the pedagogical practices of their teachers: A collaborative study.* Unpublished record of study, Texas A&M University, College Station, Texas.

Mallow, F., & Patterson, L. (1999). *Framing literacy: Teaching/learning in K–8 classrooms.* Norwood, MA: Christopher-Gordon.

Margulies, N. (1991). *Mapping inner space.* Tucson, AZ: Zephyr Press.

Martin, B. (1991). *Sounds of language readers.* Allen, TX: DLM.

Moll, L., Amanti, C., Neff, D., & Gonzalez, N. (1992). Funds of knowledge for teaching: Using a qualitative approach to connect homes and classrooms. *Theory Into Practice, 31,* 132–141.

Ogle, D. (1986). K-W-L: A teaching model that develops active reading of expository text. *The Reading Teacher, 39* (6), 564–570.

Padrón, Y. N., & Waxman, H. C. (1988). The effect of ESL students' perceptions of their congitive strategies on reading achievement. *Teachers of English as a Second Language Quarterly, 22,* 146–150.

Patterson, L., & Baldwin, S. (1999). Claiming our ignorance and making new friends. *Networks: An On-line Journal for Teacher Researchers, 2,* 2 (http://www.oise.utoronto.ca/~ctd/networks/).

Pinnell, G., & Fountas, I. (1996). *Guided reading: Good first teaching for all children.* Portsmouth, NH: Heinemann.

Pinnell, G., & Fountas, I. (1998). *Word matters.* Portsmouth, NH: Heinemann.

Smith, F. (1982). *Writing and the writer.* NY: Holt, Rinehart and Winston.

Stauffer, R. (1975). *Directing the reading-thinking process.* New York: Harper & Row.

Sulzby, E. (1985). Children's emergent reading of favorite storybooks: A developmental study. *Reading Research Quarterly, 20,* 458–481.

Sulzby, E. (1989). The development of the young child and the emergence of literacy. In J. Flood, J. Jensen, D. Lapp, & J. Squire (Eds.), *Handbook of research on teaching the English language arts* (3rd ed.) (pp. 273–285). New York: Macmillan.

Teale, W. (1986). Home background and young children's literacy development. In W. Teale & E. Sulzby (Eds.), *Emergent literacy: Writing and reading* (pp. 173–206). Norwood, NJ: Ablex Publishing Corporation.

Trelease, J. (1995). *The read-aloud handbook.* 4th Ed. New York: Penguin Books.

Van Allen, R. (1976). *Language experiences in education.* Boston: Houghton Mifflin.

Wells, G. (1981). *Learning through interaction: The study of language development.* Cambridge: Cambridge University Press.

Wilhelm, J. (1997). *You gotta be the book.* Portsmouth, NH: Heinemann.

Williams, R. (1991). *Integrated learning workshops: Launching a love of literature.* Bothell, WA: The Wright Group.

About the Authors

Dr. Leslie Patterson, left; Dr. Frances Mallow, right.

Dr. Leslie Patterson has nine years of teaching experience in public schools and fourteen years of experience in university teacher education. She is currently a professor at the University of North Texas in Denton, TX. She has served as a consultant for numerous school districts, most recently working with faculties to build schoolwide Title I programs. Her work as a teacher researcher in K–12 classrooms has yielded a number of collaborative publications, including Teacher Research: From *Promise to Power* (Richard Owen Publisher, 1990), *Teachers Are Researchers: Reflection and Action* (International Reading Association, 1993), and *Texts, Talk and Inquiry* (International Reading Association, 1996).

Dr. Frances Mallow is formerly the Director of Institution at Yeager Elementary, a suburban school with a large bilingual population in Cypress-Fairbanks Independent School District, in Houston, Texas. An educator with over 30 years in the public schools of Texas, she has served as a classroom teacher, a reading teacher, a Title I and dyslexia coordinator, and an ESL teacher for both adults and children. She has provided staff development for teachers and teaching assistants in several school districts, worked closely with teachers and children in developing new programs and has written curriculum. She has taught graduate and undergraduate courses in reading education at Sam Houston State University, Texas A&M University, and the University of Houston.

Both Leslie and Frances are from three generations of educators. Heavily influenced as readers and writers by family experiences, they also read and wrote with their children; and Frances now enjoys watching her five grandchildren and their emerging literacy.

Index

A

action research cycle, 2, 3, 6, 7
alphabetic principle, 41
art, 28, 41, 62, 65, 68, 88, 100
assessment
    of literacy strategies, 34, 54, 62, 89, 98
    phonemic awareness, 42-44, 50
assisted reading, 15, 30, 56, 94
author's chair, 34
autobiographies, 34

B

big books, 48, 49
big picture, 62, 65
bilingual classrooms, 98-103
book
    clubs, 64
    handling knowledge task, 45, 46
    introductions, 64
brainstorming, 56
building a literacy team, 105, 106

C

cartoon strips, 65
choosing
    a topic for writing, 56, 90
    appropriate books, 82
choral reading, 56
class
    expert, 34
    yearbook, 34
cloze activities, 85
cognitive processing, 12
collaborative learning experiences, 39
comprehension
    listening, 60
    strategies, 62, 63
conceptual maps, 65, 66, 67
conferences, 22, 53, 89, 90
    reading, 90
    student, 81
    writing, 89, 90

conversations,
    about literacy, 2
    about language, 93
    student, 81
    teaching, 22
    written, 58
cueing systems, 72-74

D

daily
    reading chart, 21
    writing chart, 21, 22
dance, 62
diagnostic spelling tests, 90-92
dialogue
    and inquiry process, 3
    journals, 34
dictation, 54
directed listening-thinking activity (DL-TA) assessment, 28, 29
directed reading-thinking activity (DR-TA) assessment, 29, 30
drama, 62
drawing, 28, 41, 62, 65, 68, 88, 100

E

echo reading, 56
Elkonin boxes, 50
English as a second language, 97-103
emergent literacy, 9, 10, 44, 45, 56, 83
    behavior that demonstrates, 17, 18
    characteristics of, 12-17
environmental print, 10, 11, 54, 97
    awareness inventory, 46-48
    checklist, 48

F

fast and furious writing, 58
fix-up strategies, 40
fluency, 18-20, 56
    routine for writing, 57, 59
forming literacy teams, 4-7
funds of knowledge, 103

G

getting acquainted with students, 34
goal setting, student, 82, 92, 93
graphophonemic cues, 71
ground rules for Literacy Teams, 5
guided
    reading, 15, 22, 38, 83, 84
    writing, 84, 85

H

home support 31, 40, 51, 60, 68, 86, 95, 103
how to help your child with reading, 68
hypothesis testing processes, 14

I

independent
    reading, 39
    writing, 53
individualistic development, 9
inquiry cycle, 2
interactive writing, 42, 93
interest inventory, 54, 55
    questionnaire, 55
interviews, student, 81
invented spelling, 41, 53, 54, 72

J

journals,
    dialogue, 34
    response, 64, 81
    writing, 59

K

key words, 49
kidwatching, 12, 89, 98
K-W-L chart, 38, 39

L

Language experience approach (LEA), 49, 50
learning log, 54
letter writing, 10, 59, 64, 93
leveled texts, 82

listening comprehension, 60
literacy
    events in the home, 10, 12
    strategies, assessment of, 34, 54, 62, 89, 98
literacy center activities, 31, 40, 51, 59, 60, 67, 85, 94
    alphabet center, 51
    art center, 103
    book center, 85, 86
    classroom travel agency, 40
    dialogue journal center, 94
    discovery center, 67
    environmental print big book center, 102, 103
    fast writing center, 59
    listening center, 95
    "magic glasses" center, 31
    pet hospital, 40
    "play like" center, 31
    pocket chart center, 51
    recording/reporter center, 59, 60
    word study center, 86
    writing center, 67
literacy teams
    forming, 4-7
    building, 105, 106
    ground rules for, 5
literature circles, 64

M

me museum, 34
mentor, 29
metalinguistic,
    ability, 45
    awareness, 82
    inventory, 63
    interviews, 63
mind mapping, 101, 102
modified miscue analysis, 72-80

O

ownership of learning, student, 82, 88, 92, 93
oral language, 9, 10, 42, 54, 56, 71, 72, 98

P

parent/guardian questionnaire, 34, 35
peer groups for reading and writing, 39
pen pal letters, 59
phonemic awareness, 15
    assessments, 42-44, 50
planning sheets, 6
play acting, 29
poetry, 65
portfolio reflections, student, 81
predictable text, 49, 72
prediction, 14, 39, 42, 85
    cycle, 14
print concepts, 53
prior knowledge, 14, 38, 42, 62, 72

Q

questionnaire, student, 81

R

readers' theatre, 65
reading
    assisted, 15, 30, 56, 94
    buddies, 39
    choosing appropriate books, 82
    choral, 56, 100
    conferences, 90
    daily, chart, 21
    echo, 56
    guided, 15, 22, 38, 83, 84
    how to help your child with, 68
    independent, 39
    peer groups, 39
    records, student, 81
    relationship between writing and, 53
    repeated, 94
    re-reading, 56, 72
    shared, 22, 42, 48, 49, 62
    storybook, 10, 11, 61
    strategy interview, 98, 99
    supported, 54
    sustained, silent, 15
    transcript of oral, 76-80
reflections, student, 81, 82
relationship between reading and writing,
    53

repeated reading, 94
re-enactment, 64
response
    activities, 64
    journals, 64
re-reading, 56, 72
retelling, 35, 36, 39, 62, 65, 68, 71, 73
    and miscue analysis, 74, 75
    rubric, 36
risk taking, 10, 12
rhyming words, 42, 43

S

scaffolding, 86
self
    -correction, 72
    -evaluation, 82
    -questioning, 40
    -talk, 40
shared reading, 22, 42, 48, 49, 62
sketch and guess, 65
sound-symbol relationships, 54, 84, 90
spelling,
    diagnostic tests, 90-92
    invented, 41. 53, 54, 72
story
    charts, 65
    maps, 65, 66
storybook reading, 10, 11, 61
storytelling, 29, 56
student
    conferences, 81
    conversations, 81
    goal setting, 82, 92, 93
    inquiry, 37
    interviews, 81
    logs, 81
    ownership or learning, 82, 88, 92 93
    portfolios, 81
    questionnaires, 81
    reading records, 81
    reflections, 81, 82
    response journals, 81
    self-evaluation, 82
    think alouds, 81
supported reading and writing, 54
sustained silent reading, 15

systematic data gathering and analysis, 7

T

teacher conferences, 22, 53, 89, 90
    demonstrations of writing, 55, 56
    observations, 89
teaching conversations, 22
texts, leveled, 82
think aloud, 39, 40, 81
transcript of oral reading, 7-80

W

writing
    choosing a topic for, 56, 90
    conferences, 89, 90
    conversations, 59
    daily, chart, 21, 22
    development, 10-12
    fast and furious, 58
    fluency, routine for, 57, 59
    guided, 84, 85
    independent, 53
    interactive, 42, 93
    journal, 59
    letters, 10, 59, 64, 93
    peer groups, 39
    relationship between reading and, 53
    roulette, 57
    shared, writing, 57, 62
    supported, 54
    teacher demonstrations of, 55, 56
    text for wordless picture books, 56

Y

Yopp-Singer Phonemic Awareness Test, 43, 44